#1 bestselling author

The Companies We Keep 2

**More Amazing Stories
About Hawaii's People,
Places, and Companies**

Bob Sigall

and his students at Hawaii Pacific University

The Companies We Keep 2

More Amazing Stories About Hawaii's People, Places, and Companies

© 2008 by Bob Sigall

First Edition

Published by:

Small Business Hawaii
6600 Kalanianaole Highway #212
Honolulu, Hawaii 96825
808-396-1724

Send comments, new stories and corrections to:

CompaniesWeKeep@Yahoo.com
Visit our web site at: www.CompaniesWeKeep.com

ISBN # 0-9724504-1-6

Cover designed by Debra Castro

Book layout and design by David Walker

Printed in Hong Kong by Imaging Hawaii

Duke Kahanamoku and Babe Ruth hang out in Waikiki in 1937. Bishop Museum photo.

What people are saying about
'The Companies We Keep'

"If you like to read this column, let me suggest a book you might enjoy: **The Companies We Keep**, by Bob Sigall. It's loaded with oddball information about Our Honolulu."

—**Bob Krauss**, *Honolulu Advertiser*

"One of the most fascinating Hawaii books in a long time."

—**Perry & Price**, KSSK radio

"**The Companies We Keep** is a fascinating book that, if not on your bookshelf, should be. It's a kamaaina-must-have."

—*MidWeek*

"An enlightening and entertaining book, with thousands of intriguing tidbits."

—*Hawaii* magazine

"People in Hawaii will find it a nostalgic trip down memory lane. It's a Kamaaina trivia lovers delight."

—**Honolulu Star-Bulletin**

"History and nostalgia that is thoroughly engaging."

—*Spirit of Aloha* magazine

"**The Companies We Keep** is a perfect gift for longtime Hawaii residents or someone who has moved to the mainland."

—*Hawaii Reporter*

Table of Contents

Table of Contents

Table of Contents

Table of Contents

Table of Contents

The Royal Hawaiian Hotel in 1968, before the Sheraton Hotel was built next door. Hawaii State Archives photo.

A Special Mahalo

To my wife, Lei. You're the best thing that ever happened to me.

My parents, Sol and Martha Sigall, who have supported everything I've ever done.

Julie Percell for inspiring my first book with stories of Arakawa's and Liberty House.

Rich Budnick, my mentor in self-publishing.

All my HPU students who did research for the book.

Editors: Brandi Boatner, Cathy Handen, and Jara Takahashi

The Pau Hana Pumpers: Dean Kaneshiro, Wanda Nakamura, Herb Hamada, Mel and Theo Fujiyoshi, Brian Walthall, Van Lee, Craig and Karen Arakawa, and the staff at CHART.

Sam Slom and the Board of Small Business Hawaii.

DeSoto Brown and the staff of the Bishop Museum.

Luella Kurkjian and the staff of the Hawaii State Archives.

Barbara Dunn and the staff of the Hawaiian Historical Society.

Local bookstore owners Brian Melzack at Bestsellers, Pat Banning at Bookends, and managers at Borders, Barnes & Noble and Native Books/Na Mea Hawaii.

The staff of the Hawaii State Library system, particularly David Del Rocco.

Restaurants that sell the book, including Boulevard Saimin, Helena's Hawaiian Food, Gyotaku, Hungry Lion, Da Big Kahuna's, Highway Inn, and Flamingo.

The members of Rotary District 5000.

The HawaiiThreads.com community for ideas and inspiration.

Andy Poepoe, Jane Sawyer, and the staff of the U.S. Small Business Administration, the Small Business Development Center, and the Women in Business Committee.

Honolulu Advertiser Editor Mark Platte, and Library staff: Elyse Smout, Zenaida Cadaoas, Sonnie Rodrigues, Mildred Yoshimura, Gail Soranaka, Ken Nakakura, Redentor Sales, and Carolyn Noah.

Fact checking: Mayor Mufi-Hannemann, and Joe Moore.

Also, Pam Chambers, Jed Gaines, Barbara Campbell, Stacy Tritt, Kitty Lagareta, Michael W. Perry, Larry Price, Bob Krauss, Kathleen Severini, Bill Ogawa, Jeff Cook, Steve Sugai, Dennis Momyer, and Sean Morris.

Your support made a huge difference. Thank you all.

Mahalo to Our Sponsors

Many individuals and companies have come forward to support the publication of this book, and we wish to thank:

Small Business Hawaii
Creating a better Hawaii
through private enterprise

Barron Guss, ALTRES HR and ALTRES Staffing
Hawaii's premier providers
of human resources services

Andy's Pool and Spa Services
Complete pool & spa care services
to Oahu residents since 1979

Helena's Hawaiian Food
A James Beard Regional
Award winning restaurant

Da Big Kahuna's Pizza and Stuffs
Da buggahs are loaded

Sol and Martha Sigall
Happily married for
over 61 years

An Aesop's Fable

The donkey

A MAN WISHED TO PURCHASE A DONKEY, and agreed with its owner that he should try out the animal before he bought him. He took the donkey home and put him in the straw-yard with his other donkeys, upon which the new animal left all the others and at once joined the one that was most idle and the laziest of them all.

Seeing this, the man put a halter on him and led him back to his owner. On being asked how, in so short a time, he could have made a trial of him, he answered, "I do not need a trial; I know that he will be just the same as the one he chose for his companion."

A man is known by the company he keeps.

This 2500-year-old Greek fable inspired the title of this book.

Hawaii is known or defined by the companies we have kept through our patronage, and the people we have embraced with our aloha.

Here are some of their stories.

Introduction

IN 2004, AN ASSIGNMENT I gave my students six years earlier at HPU, to teach them the value of networking, turned into a book. I required them to interview company owners. However, something unexpected happened.

They uncovered dozens of fascinating stories about Hawaii companies, schools and organizations. By the fourth semester of the networking assignment, I typed up several pages of what the students had discovered. I had a few extra copies I gave to friends, who were wowed by the information. It was then I realized we might have material worthy of being published.

The Companies We Keep presented what my students had learned in meeting with business owners over ten semesters. They did much of the interviews with existing Oahu companies. I researched neighbor island companies, schools; and organizations that were based on the mainland, or were no longer in business.

Because of the reaction of my friends, I had a feeling the book would do well, but I never imagined it would make the bestseller list, let alone reach #1.

I did hope that the book would connect me with other great Hawaii stories, and that did happen. This second volume is the result. Some of the stories are about Hawaii companies and organizations, but more are about people and places.

For instance, Joe Moore told me his secret to longevity and success. Perry & Price explained how they are "just one phone call away from greatness." Frank De Lima described what Imelda Marcos said about his impersonation of her.

I discovered a local organization was founded because of an *Oprah* show. Shirley Temple met her husband in Hawaii. Marilyn Monroe told a *Star-Bulletin* reporter here in 1954 about the first time she felt like a star.

The thread that ties all the stories together in this and the previous book is that they are amazing stories about Hawaii — stories the public is largely unaware of about people, places, companies, and organizations.

Steve Sugai of Shiatsu Therapists of Hawaii recalled a contest to name Magic Island, when I showed him pictures before it had been built. This sent me to the Hawaii State Library, where I found a list of names they considered, including Duke Kahanamoku Park.

Even more intriguing was a 1969 photo of a model of what Henry Kaiser first proposed. Could the *Honolulu Advertiser* still have that photo, I wondered. Within 2 minutes of my call, they found the picture. I discovered that they have the second-largest photo collection in the state, and it's very well organized. Most of the pictures in this second book are from their archives.

If you know of other great Hawaii stories, errors or omissions, email them to us at:

CompaniesWeKeep@Yahoo.com.

We'll include some of them on our web site, which is at:

www.CompaniesWeKeep.com.

Here are more of the stories you'll find in this book:

John Rodgers Airport was named for the man who flew his seaplane 2,000 miles to Hawaii, in 1925 but ran out of fuel. His crew made sails from the wings' fabric and sailed the remaining 350 miles here.

Elvis first came to Hawaii after receiving 21,000 Christmas cards in 1956.

Four major sports were created by people who lived in Hawaii — surfing, basketball, baseball and volleyball.

One man predicted in 1923 that Japan would bomb Pearl Harbor, before aircraft carriers, using Niihau as a base.

A fisherman, blown off course in 1844 became the first Japanese visitor to Hawaii. He returned to help Commodore Perry negotiate with Japan, and was made a samurai as a reward.

Sports legend Jackie Robinson played semi-pro football in Hawaii in 1941 before breaking baseball's color barrier.

A huge replica of Iolani Palace was built out of snow at the Sapporo Snow Festival in 1982.

How wallabies came to Kalihi Valley.

Why the Bishop Estate once considered moving to South Dakota.

Kui Lee wrote *I'll remember you* for his wife, Nani, who left him after a stormy marriage.

Former Mayor Neal Blaisdell once pitched for the Baltimore Orioles.

The U.H. "Rainbows" nickname was given by reporters when a rainbow appeared during a game, soon followed by a touchdown.

What did Imelda Marcos think about Frank De Lima's impression of her?

What do you do when the person you're impersonating comes to see your show? Honolulu Advertiser *photos.*

HAWAII'S GREATEST, most outrageous comedian isn't afraid to go out on a limb for a laugh. He's been known to do Mufi Hannemann, standing on a stool with a bad wig. Tina Turner? Fair game. Elvis? Why not?

But what happens, when they come to see your show? That's what happened to the Portuguese Prince of Hawaiian Comedy, Frank De Lima. Imelda came to see him one night.

Patrick Downes, one of De Lima's writers, says Frank was very nervous, but he plugs right ahead. "Imelda is a parody of herself, and she must think she's being flattered, and can laugh at herself."

"Jim Nabors brought Imelda and Doris Duke to see the show," De Lima recalls. "I came out dressed like her, with the black sunglasses with gold trim, the puffy shoulders, and shoes and the audience roared for a good five minutes." Imelda talked to him afterwards and said she liked the show. "She said she couldn't believe how much I looked like her!"

De Lima's career has spanned decades. Patrick Downes says he first met Frank at St. Stephen's Seminary in the 1960s. "We formed a musical group, Hui o Hawaii, with Frank leading on ukulele, me on guitar, and several others. We played the standards and backed up the hula troupe. It was a lot of fun."

"Frank is a natural performer," Downes says. "He could relate to people and make them laugh. He developed many comedy routines, such as KOHO radio, which was a take off on a real radio station. He'd tell Portuguese jokes and do local accents."

De Lima left the seminary in his last year. "I don't think he was made for the priesthood. He was developing as an entertainer, and could see his whole life moving in that direction. A job singing at tour briefings led to a lounge act in Waikiki."

Frank De Lima in the 8th grade was already impersonating his neighbors.

Hula Records' Flip McDiarmid caught one of his shows and suggested a comedy album. The result was *A taste of Malasadas* recorded live at the Noodle Shop in 1978.

"Frank asked me to write the liner notes," Downes recalls. "I included a humorous recipe for char siu malasadas. It was pretty gross. I put two recipes together, and discovered comedy in juxtaposing two things that don't normally go together. It makes people think twice."

"The album was a hit and when the time came for a second record, Frank had used up all the material he developed since high school. There was nothing left, so I said let me help you. That's how we began writing together."

"One of the first things I wrote was *Abdulla Fata'ai* - a name we made up about a guy that walked with a turban in Hauula. I never even knew the guy. It was just a fun name. I told Frank he had established himself as an ethnic comedian, with Japanese and Chinese accents. Are you ready to tackle Samoans?"

The song made fun of "mokes" or "large, brawl-prone Polynesian men." On stage, Frank hung breadfruit around his neck and carried a rubber club. The song was a huge hit.

By then, De Lima was doing 2-3 shows a night at the Noodle Shop, with sold-out crowds and lines around the block. "He killed. People were rolling in the aisles with laughter. The show gave him leeway to learn the craft, make a bunch of mistakes, learn what worked and what didn't."

"Frank doesn't sit down and write," Downes says "He thinks things up and perfects it on stage. He comes up with an idea and I'd develop it. Or I'd come up with stuff."

"Most of his creativity comes as he works an idea in his mind or on stage. In the 1980s I'd give him raw material and he'd transform it. Through audience interaction, it becomes his and it's always an improvement, always funnier. He has an innate sense of humor and can tickle the funny bone of his audience."

"I just help him out with the lyrics, punch lines. If I did it on stage, it would be a total failure. If he did it himself, he'd run out of material. So we're a good team," Downes believes.

"At some point, we began developing characters, like Mary Tunta, Pocho Man, Tita Turner, Cardinal Vermicelli, and Imelda. Once we had a successful character, like Imelda, I'd write for the character, not for Frank. It became easy to riff on her shoes or her love of dressing up or something. We'd milk it for all it was worth." Tremaine Tamayose wrote this to *I left my heart in San Francisco*.

I left my shoes, in my Manila.
I left my bras and my panties too.
When I come home to you, my Filipinos
I'll wear my shoes to walk on you.

"He did two full-on productions at the Waikiki Shell with musicians, smoke, lighting, and Frank was as outrageous as he could be. He wore huge headdresses that lit up, and swung from a swing that lowered from the top of the Shell. It lost money, but it was a childhood dream, and he didn't care."

"I felt a freedom to write and experiment. I wrote a serious song called *Waimea Lullaby*. It was well-arranged with an oboe, and violins. We didn't really know what we were doing. Frank recorded it and it won a 1980 Hoku Award as Song of the Year. It blew us all away. We were on cloud nine. We felt we could do anything — comedy and serious songs. The next album was half

and half and bombed. *Waimea Lullaby* was a fluke. We returned to pure comedy after that."

"I caught Jerry Santos singing *Lucille* ("You picked a fine time to leave me, Lucille ...) and thought it was very funny. I thought, what if Frank sang it? He would be even funnier:"

What! Luceel, you goin' leave me now?
The kids nevah eat yet! Mango season not pau.
I know my car stay smokin'
And da stereo stay broken, but wow, lau lau
What! Luceel, you goin' leave me now?

Frank De Lima with Na Kolohe: Dean Lum and Dean Shimabukuro at the Noodle Shop in 1983.

"*Glen Miyashiro* is about the generic Japanese male. It's set to the song *Guantanamera*. I'm married to a Japanese woman, so I took aspects of my in-laws, which she didn't appreciate too much at the time. She's fine with it now. My cousin married a Glen."

My name is Glen Miyashiro
I went to Kaimuki High School
And I went UH Manoa
And I wen' work in one office
And I went and got married
We got reception at Kapiolani Hotel

"He's interchangeable with any Japanese male and is a boring person. It's funny because a lot of it is true."

Downes says Perry & Price actually had a contest to see who most fit the character. "People come up to me and say, 'I know who you're talking about; I know who Glen is,' I say, no you don't."

Before naming the character, Downes went to the phone book to see how many Glen Miyashiro's there were. There were only two. "I didn't want a name too many real people had."

"I was in Longs in Waipahu," De Lima recalls, "and this woman told me her husband was one of the real Glen Miyashiro's. They got so many calls at 2 AM, they unlisted their number!"

"Frank's comedy is more like family humor. Every Hawaii family has a Portuguese godmother, a Filipino son-in-law, or a Japanese mother-in-law; it's all mixed. Writing for Frank is like finding humor in your own family. It's like making fun of your brother's cooking and finding a receptive audience, because it's an inside joke. Frank uses inside-Hawaii family jokes. Almost literally, we're all family.

"Frank is Portuguese, Hawaiian, Irish, Chinese, English, Spanish, and Scottish. No Japanese. He wishes he had Japanese. He has a definite affection for them."

For twenty-five years, De Lima has visited local schools. He visits every public and private school statewide every two years.

"It began with Kahului Elementary school in 1980 and has grown from there," De Lima says. "I was inspired by *Captain Kangaroo* and Mr. Greenjeans who entertained kids on TV, but also talked to them about life. I thought maybe I could do that too."

For kindergarten through third grade, Frank's message is that the foundation for a well-rounded life is reading, studying, laughing and family. "We need all four to be happy."

For fourth grade and up, the Frank De Lima Student Enrichment Program changes the message. "This year and next, the message is responsibility. I use my career as an example. A lot of my CD's are song parodies, but I have to get permission to use a song, and sometimes they say no. I wanted to do that with the song *Bad Day*. But sometimes when you want something, the answer is no. It's a fact of life."

De Lima has recently lost 100 pounds as part of being responsible for his own health.

Patrick Downes says, "the program is his way of giving back. He loves kids and is very committed to this. He gets some grants now, but has poured his own money into it for 20 years. He feels it's something he has to do."

Already set up

Frank has the advantage that he has developed himself into a personality. With a lot of hard work, he's established himself as a funny guy.

"The advantage to that is that he can go up to a microphone and say 'testing, testing' and the audience will roar, because with comedy, you have to set people up for the punch line. All jokes have a set up and then you punch them with something unexpected."

"With Frank, they're already set up. It's much easier for him to make people laugh because people are primed already," Downes says "and he knows how to do it. He doesn't even need funny lines, just appropriate words that fit a situation and he'll have people laughing."

Larry Price says, "Frank De Lima is not just a comedian, he's a humorist. He can make anything funny. He can tell an ordinary story and make people laugh. He comes to the John Dominis show and tells a joke, but forgets the punch line, and it's better than the joke. How many guys can pull that off?"

"He ends up yelling at the audience," Michael W. Perry says. "What? Shut up! It's hilarious. Here's the Portuguese seminary student who gets away with making fun of literally every single ethnic group in the state of Hawaii. He does it with good humor and makes every one of them laugh."

De Lima and Downes are working on an album at the moment. There's a parody of *Green Acres*, a song about Ed Case running against Dan Akaka, and a parody of *Take a Walk in the Country*. Cardinal Vermicelli will make an appearance, and Mary Tunta will be running for governor.

"Frank's a personable kind of guy," Downes concludes. "Everybody knows him and greets him when we're eating at Zippy's. He's never annoyed. He knows, if not for them, he wouldn't be successful. That's why people are fond of him. He genuinely likes people."

Which group that helps Hawaii tourists was inspired by an Oprah show?

IN THE SPRING OF 1993, A BAKERSFIELD College professor, Chuck Wall, heard a news story on the radio that said: "We have another random act of senseless violence to report."

In a split second, he had an idea. "I just took out the word 'violence' and stuck in the word 'kindness,'" Wall said. "All of a sudden, I had a great phrase that turned a negative into a positive."

Wall challenged his human relations class to commit one random act of senseless kindness a day. The students jumped into it, and later printed bumper stickers that said: "Today, I will commit one random act of senseless KINDNESS ... Will you?"

A year later, Wall was on the *Oprah* show and the phrase became known around the globe. Millions of people were inspired, including the Rotary Club of Honolulu, which created a Random Acts of Aloha Committee in 1997 to help tourists who were victims of crime or other adversities.

The committee became an independent non-profit organization named the Visitor Aloha Society of Hawaii. Its mission is to deal with visitors who are the victim of crime or adversity and turn their experience into a more positive one, so they could leave with an upbeat memory of Hawaii.

Seven million tourists visit Hawaii each year, and for a small number, tragedy strikes. Many of these tourists would return home to tell their friends how horrible Hawaii was, and this could hurt our economy.

"We can't change what has happened," says Executive Director

Jessica Rich, "but we can certainly step in and lend a hand."

Many visitors think shoes are a safe, and put money, credit cards, and car keys in it on the beach. They return from a swim to find the contents gone.

One man dug a hole in the sand, put

An Oprah show inspired the creation of the Visitor Aloha Society of Hawaii. Wikipedia Commons photo by Alan Light.

his valuables in it, and drew an arrow to it. When he returned it was gone. Some leave thousands of dollars on the beach unattended.

An 18-year old woman left her purse on her towel with all the money for her wedding in it. It was stolen and she was really upset. "The police called us," Rich says. "We can't replace what they lost. We're not an insurance company, but we were able to get her an ocean view hotel room and meal vouchers. She was very pleased that someone came to her rescue."

Many tourists leave their valuables in the car. Over 300 visitors a year on Oahu are shocked to find their cameras, tickets, and cash are gone when they return from lunch.

"Some of them are saying 'I hate Hawaii,' when we first show up. Later they have turned around and they end up with a positive feeling about the people of Hawaii."

The Visitor Aloha Society is called on by the police, hospitals, hotels, and rental car agencies. They provide hotel rooms, transportation, meal vouchers, clothes, entertainment, legal assistance, and help getting passports to about 1,000 visitors in need a year.

To put that in perspective, 99.95% of visitors to the islands have a positive, uneventful time here. The Visitor Aloha Society is there for that tiny fraction that isn't so fortunate.

"I got called to a hotel where a grandmother had died in her sleep. The family was traumatized and didn't know what to do. We helped them with arrangements and legal papers. They later wrote 'your kindness, compassion, professionalism and even gifts for the children did much to help us emotionally during such a difficult time.'"

"They don't look at Hawaii as a bad place," Rich comments, "but as a place where there was an out-pouring of support for them."

On another occasion, one volunteer helped a woman who broke her hip on a cruise. Her friends continued around the islands, but she was hospitalized at Straub. "Our volunteer showed up and visited her every day. This woman said she could never have gone through the experience if not for our volunteer visiting and helping her. We took away her feelings of isolation."

"When we show up in people's darkest hours, there's a transformation. A heart to heart caring develops between two strangers, and when they get back home, that is what they remember."

The Visitor Aloha Society has two full time staff, five part-time, and about 80 volunteers. The Hawaii Tourism Authority is one contributor, but thousands in the community also donate.

"Members of the visitor industry provide the hotel rooms, air fares, taxis, meals, tickets to events, etc., out of their kindness and concern for our visitors," says Visitor Aloha board chairperson Dr. Terry Wade. "When you see the totality of the efforts by all of these people, you can't help but believe in the Aloha Spirit."

The Visitor Aloha Society provides an invaluable service to those in need, but they also help everyone in the state by protecting Hawaii's reputation. Every one of us benefits in some way from tourism, which represents at least a third of our economy.

"Police officers appreciate the Visitor Aloha Society," says HPD Captain Jeffrey Richards. The burden of caring for visitors who were victims of crime often fell on police who were untrained in this area. "It gives officers another avenue or place to turn with this type of problem."

Terry Wade calls Jessica Rich "the model executive director for visitor assistance programs everywhere. All of us in Hawaii, as well as the many visitors she assists from all over the world, are blessed to have someone who is so completely devoted to helping people and who is exceptionally good at it. She is an embodiment of the Aloha Spirit."

"The majority of people we help are just amazed that Hawaii has an organization that just shows up when they need it," Rich says, "like a best friend, who is there when you most need them."

Wade tells the volunteers during training sessions that visitors who come to Hawaii and are victims of crime and other adversities, suffer losses. The biggest loss, however, is the expectation of visiting paradise and receiving Aloha.

"We cannot replace their property, and we certainly cannot bring back loved ones. But we can extend the Aloha Spirit to them, and we thereby hope to restore what I consider the most important gift we can offer to people in this troubled world."

And all this was inspired by an *Oprah* show.

How The U.H. Rainbows
got their nickname

FOR THEIR FIRST 14 YEARS, THE NICKNAME OF the University of Hawaii sports teams was drastically different than we know them today. They were called the Fighting Deans. That might be because faculty played on the first teams.

The University of Hawaii was founded in 1907 as the College of Agriculture and Mechanic Arts. It occupied temporary quarters across from Thomas Square on Victoria, Young and Beretania Streets. The Manoa campus wasn't ready until 1912.

Sharing the space on the same property was McKinley High School. The building that now houses the Academy of Arts Annex was built for McKinley, which didn't move into their current campus until 1923.

In 1909, the Fighting Deans played its first football game — against McKinley High School. They won 6-5 before a crowd of 2,500 at Punahou School.

Wait a second. Did a college play a high school? It sounds crazy, but UH didn't play against another college until 1920, when they lost to the University of Nevada. UH didn't have an all-college schedule until 1966! Besides, high schools, UH played military, clubs, and other adult teams.

Coach Otto "Proc" Klum took over as UH coach in 1921. His quarterback that year was Mayor-to-be Neal S. Blaisdell. He led the Fighting Deans to their first winning season the following year, which included their first win against another college, Cal Poly Pomona.

For his prowess as a coach, Klum was given the nickname "Manoa

Legendary Otto "Proc" Klum was called the "Manoa Fox." He coached at UH from 1921 to 1939. UH Photo.

Fox." Klum Gym was named for him 30 years later, in 1956, and one source says it was called "the Madison Square Garden of the Pacific" when it opened.

On January 1, 1923, Oregon State University traveled to Hawaii for a game at Moiliili Field. Late in the fourth quarter, the score was tied at 0-0 when a rainbow appeared over the field. UH soon scored and the sportswriters began calling the team the "Rainbows." Fans believed we would win if a rainbow appeared.

Perhaps the greatest teams in UH football history were the 1924-25 season's "Wonder Teams." The 1924 team had UH's first perfect (8-0) record and only allowed their opponents to score 12 points all season. In 1925, the Rainbows had a 10-0 season and held its opponents to only 17 points.

In those 18 games, the Rainbows defeated Washington State, Colorado, and Colorado State and outscored their opponents 606-29.

The football team's nickname changed in the 1960s to Rainbow Warriors when the school newspaper ridiculed the nickname Rainbows, saying terms like that were used by homosexuals.

In 2000, the football team dropped "Rainbow" and became "Warriors" at coach June Jones' urging.

What convinced Elvis to come to Hawaii?

ELVIS AND HIS MANAGER, COL. TOM PARKER, considered a Hawaii concert in 1956, but thought the population was too small to sell out two shows.

However, in December of that year, Hawaii residents sent the 21 year old Elvis Presley 21,000 Christmas cards, demonstrating boundless interest in the King of Rock and Roll.

Two concerts were held at the old Honolulu Stadium on November 10, 1957. The most expensive seats were $3.50 (about $25 in today's dollars).

There have been thousands of Elvis impersonators, but the very first one was in Hawaii. Tom Moffatt dressed Donn Tyler, a KHVH staff member in an Elvis wig, and put him in the back seat of a white convertible next to a Col. Parker impersonator. Ron Jacobs drove them around the island the day before the concert. Moffatt reported their "whereabouts" on the radio. Honolulu was hysterical with sightings.

Elvis returned for a second concert in 1961 – his first after getting out of the Army. His concert at the Bloch Arena raised $50,000 to help build the USS Arizona Memorial.

His 1973 "Aloha From Hawaii" concert was the first to be broadcast via satellite. Over one billion people watched.

Over 1 billion saw Elvis' Aloha From Hawaii concert, televised from the Honolulu International Center in 1973.

Left: Elvis received 21,000 Christmas cards from Hawaii in 1956, which convinced him to come here in 1957. Honolulu Advertiser photos.

Did the Miss America Pageant block an Asian Miss Hawaii from participating?

The Miss America Pageant gave Miss Hawaii, Yun Tau Zane, an exemption to compete in 1948. Honolulu Advertiser *photos.*

THE MISS America Pageant did have a Rule #7 that stipulated "contestants must be of good health and of the white race." However, when the first Miss Hawaii pageant was held in 1948, the Hawaii organizers were able to obtain an exemption from the Miss America Pageant.

Twenty year-old Yun Tau Zane, a sophomore at the University of Hawaii entered the contest that was part of the very first 49th State Fair held in 1948 at Kapiolani Park. At the time, Hawaii expected to be the 49th state, hence the name of the fair.

Irmgard Waiwaiole won the pageant but later relinquished her crown because she had not graduated from high school. Like many others, World War II had interrupted her education. Runner-up Yun Tau Zane was named Miss Hawaii, and became the first Asian American to compete for the Miss America title.

Zane danced the hula for the talent portion of the contest. Although she didn't win, she was voted Miss Congeniality, which came with a $1,000 scholarship. Miss Hawaii used the money to earn her teaching certificate from the University of Wisconsin. She taught at Maemae School for 26 years.

Hawaii girls were named Miss Congeniality three times in the first four years they participated in the Miss America Pageant.

The Miss America tournament grew out of a city-wide festival in Atlantic City to boost tourism after Labor Day. The festival was called the "Fall Frolic,"

Yun Tau Zane was the first Miss Hawaii in 1948.

which included an "Inter-City Beauty Contest."

The first Asian American to become Miss America, was Hawaii's Angela Perez Baraquio, who won in 2001

Many King Street drivers have noticed that there's a Miss Hawaii Building across the street from Zippy's near Washington Intermediate. It actually has no relation to the pageant.

The Miss Hawaii Building dates to 1947 when Genjira Jinbo was part owner of the Miss Hawaii Manufacturing Company which made women's clothing. This was a year before the Miss Hawaii Pageant began.

Yun Tau Zane was voted Miss Congeniality.

33

Whose idea was Magic Island?

IT WAS HENRY KAISER WHO FIRST PROPOSED building Magic Island, in 1955. Kaiser "retired" to Hawaii but he was a visionary. He looked at Maunalua and developed it into what we, today, call Hawaii Kai. He took the Niumalu Hotel and turned it into Kaiser's Hawaiian Village Hotel. He began KHVH radio and TV, now called KITV.

Before Ala Moana Center was built, the beach park was little used. Back in 1950, few lived in the area. Tourism was still

Before Magic Island was built, the view of Diamond Head from Ala Moana beach was stunning, as this 1955 Honolulu Advertiser *photo shows.*

Henry Kaiser built a model to show his ideas for Magic Island, including the peninsula we know today, two real islands between it, and Kewalo Basin, bridges, inlets, walkways, and six hotels. Honolulu Advertiser *photo.*

recovering from World War II and Ala Moana Center was 9 years from opening.

In 1947, Public Works Superintendent Ben Rush suggested new land for hotels and residences could be reclaimed from the ocean.

Henry Kaiser envisioned a huge development for tourists and locals. He proposed building the peninsula that we call Magic Island today. He also wanted to build two large islands parallel to the beach, with inlets for boats and pedestrian bridges. And it was he who coined the name Magic Island.

Kaiser offered to pay the $50 million cost if the City and State allowed him to build six hotels on the property.

It was a huge political issue for almost 10 years. Finally the state decided to limit the project and pay for it with public funds. Magic Island was completed in 1972, when its grand opening was held.

A *Star-Bulletin* poll gathered possible names for the project, including Duke Kahanamoku Park, Ala Moana Island, Leapuna (coral promontory), Kuikahi, (peaceful, quiet), Mokuokala (island of the sun), and Moku Lealea (pleasure island).

The 50th State Fair was held on Magic Island as it was being built and before trees were planted. Honolulu Advertiser *photo.*

How did an Aku-head become Pupule?

Hal Lewis was given the nickname "Aku-head" by an irate listener, when he gave the wrong time on air, sending her running to the office an hour early.

H AL LEWIS said it began with a simple mistake in 1947 on KPOA (now KORL) radio. "After I had been on the air a few days with my first Honolulu show I gave the wrong time one morning by mistake. I said it was an hour later than it really was."

"The next morning an irate lady with a local accent called up. She said, 'what's the matter with you? Yesterday you told me it was 8 o'clock when it was only 7. I ran out my house. When I got to work nobody was there for one hour. I got so excited I forgot to put on my pants. I no listen to you any more. You're an aku-head.'"

"I told the story on the air," Lewis continued. "Some guy called up and said 'aku-head is a good name for you.' I'd been there such a short time, I didn't realize the implication. I just thought it sounded funny."

"It started out as Akuhead and later I added pupule (crazy). Even later, I decided the name needed some dignity. So I added the initial J., which stands for nothing."

"I think that name was worth its weight in gold." Aku has no idea who the woman was. "She never called again."

Who was Aku?

Aku was the top DJ in the islands from 1947 until his death in 1983. He was the highest-paid DJ in the world, according to several sources. He was born on April 14, 1917 as Herschel Laib

Aku was the first in Hawaii to take calls on the radio. Honolulu Advertiser *photos.*

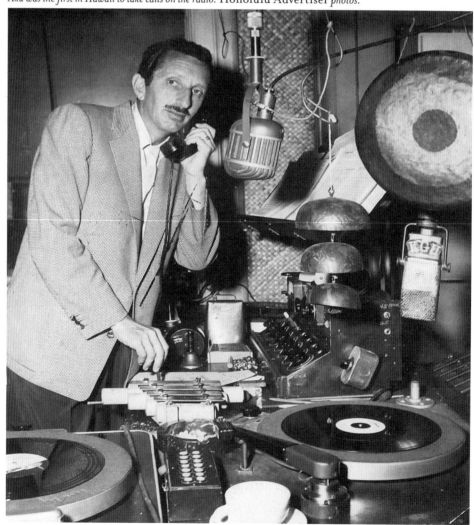

Hohenstein. By the time he came to Hawaii as a violinist on the *Matsonia*, he had changed it to Hal Lewis.

Aku was one of the first to take phone calls on the air. "Hello dere," he would say. Listeners would ask about current events or tell him jokes. He took calls from President Nixon, Sammy Davis Jr., Frank Sinatra, and Joan Crawford. He had an array of bells, whistles, buzzers, and sound effects to provide color.

When the Rock and Roll era washed over the radio waves, Aku stuck with classical and Big Band music. His 100,000 daily listeners stuck with him.

In 1973, advertising rates for Aku's broadcast were $15-25 per 30 second commercial. Today, on Perry & Price's show, rates are $200-300.

Aku pranks

Aku loved to play pranks on his listeners. In 1954, he announced that Statehood had been approved by Congress, and to apologize to islanders for waiting so many years, they could get a refund on their 1953 taxes if they filled out an application that was in the two newspapers that day. Hundreds called the IRS office or poured over the newspaper many times searching for that coupon, until told it was April 1st and a prank.

His most famous prank was an announced Easter parade down Kalakaua Avenue, on April 1. He described the floats, paniolo on horseback, and marching bands from the studio, as it passed by, in his mind. Hundreds of people showed up on Kalakaua with beach chairs and coolers to wait for a parade that never happened.

In an effort to promote the first Hawaiian Open golf tournament, Aku held a contest. Listeners had to guess how many strokes it would take him to putt from KGMB to the Waialae Country

Club. Aku wore an outlandish costume and led a procession of 50 cars and trucks.

"It took me 99 strokes and I broke 11 putters," Aku recounted. "At the end, Jack Lord appeared and put me under arrest. 'Book 'em, Danno,' he said. Then a golfer came up to hit me in the face with a pie, but I positioned myself so that when he threw it, I ducked and Lord got it in the face."

A farewell to his fans

Aku said that Hawaii had been very good to him. "Before I came here, I wasn't enjoying my life. I'm very grateful to the people of Hawaii who have made my life successful in emotional terms." The top-paid DJ in the country went on to say that "I'm not all that interested in money. I would do what I do for $3 a week, because I enjoy what I do."

Aku wrote a letter to his listeners to be read after his death.

"Folks, the news is, I didn't make it. Last Friday I went to Queens for a nuclear medicine radioactive scan. It showed that the damn cancer had jumped to the left lung, which means I'm in the group — well like I said — I didn't make it."

"Now hold on: I know it's a sad piece of news and I'm sorry to lay it on you this way, but for some reason I feel up about it rather than down. No, I do not know why I feel up. One of the main factors is the hundreds and hundreds of cards and letters from you all — with love and prayers, and all your talk-story notes about things we did together over the years."

"The positive vibrations all those messages set up created the force — the force of contentment, well being and peace that surrounds me now. After all, at 66, I've had a damn good life. Those of you folks who've been hanging with Aku in the mornings for the past 36 years know that my life has been a rich and rewarding experience. And the hundreds and thousands of you were the ones who made it possible — Hell! — You shared it with me."

"Wouldn't it be great if there really was a big golf course in the sky — and folks really could wind up playing there. That's the thought I'm holding for whenever my time is up down here. And folks, I wish there was some way I could make you know how much I have loved you all through the years."

"Folks, the news is, I didn't make it," Aku wrote in a letter to be read to his listeners.

One tearful caller to Perry & Price the following morning said she wanted to thank him for all the mornings we had breakfast together. "It's amazing you can sit down and cry for someone you've never met," she said.

Over 24 years in the top spot

PERRY & PRICE HAVE BEEN THE TOP-RANKED morning drive radio show in Honolulu for 24 years. They began the same day that Kilauea began erupting on the Big Island — August 9, 1983.

Their ratings are often equal to the next five stations combined. They have the same circulation as the newspapers.

Listeners might think they're reading the paper or relaxing during songs, and endlessly repeat the news, weather and traffic every fifteen minutes. We sat down with them after their Saturday show at John Dominis to find out what accounts for their success.

Just one phone call away from greatness

Perry: We're one phone call from greatness. We're hoping for that one call that will cause a cascade of other calls and opinions.

Price: That's what it takes in the radio business. The big trick with the phone calls is not to talk to the people who want to talk. You want to get the people who don't want to talk, to talk.

There are 100 people waiting to call us on a Monday morning and tell us what they think about something for some hidden agenda they may have; or someone they want to support. That's not the person you want to talk to.

Perry: Normal people, catching them off guard, giving you an honest description of what's happening in traffic, where they can't believe what's going on. And they tell you like they're talking to their best friend. That's the best radio there is.

Price: There's something really intimate about that phone receiver. It's something coming from their heart. It's a heartwarming kind of thing. We get a lot of that. We're lucky.

Perry: It changed my life at KKUA when we started taking phone calls. Before that, we were just a music station. I was talking just 17 seconds before playing *Shambala*.

Price: The KSSK Perry & Price Show is a team thing. We'd be dead without our team. One person can't handle that many phone calls and things. Nobody screens our calls. We answer the phones while songs are playing, but we hand them off, if we think they don't need to be on-air. We have six seconds to decide what to put on the air.

Our staff is kind of an 'Action Line.' People call with everything from lost wallets to potholes, to medical questions. We're information brokers, a referral service. We have a list of every phone number to help people. Mike knows every website known to man.

Perry: Our filter for which calls to put on the air is: is this going to be universally appealing? That's the one thing — will it be

KSSK's Perry & Price have ruled the Honolulu morning airwaves for over 24 years.

interesting to everybody else? It usually comes down to a few things: Traffic, health, simple, or perceived evils — that's great radio.

How the posse started

Price: It started out with lost pets. We used the citizens' posse thing on pet patrol. A caller told us his cocker spaniel was missing in Makiki. We'd ask the public to keep an eye out and, we'd get calls, yeah I saw him on Wilder Avenue. We went from lost pets to lost people. Finding Alzheimer's patients.

Perry: Our first posse bust was our best. This guy called in from a Fast Stop. He left the car running and went in to buy cigarettes. He came out; the car was not there anymore. He can see it heading down King Street. He calls Perry & Price. Whatever made him call Perry & Price I have no idea. We never did find out.

What kind of car is it, we asked? Toyota. License plate number? A few minutes later, a caller said he was right next to him on King Street. Pretty soon we had a group of people literally flanking this guy. They followed him all the way to a pool hall on Ala Moana. The cops busted him two minutes later.

Price: Another guy stole a car and parked it out in front of Kmart and went in to buy something. They were having a Blue Light Special. But all the guys who went for the Blue Light Special had heard about it from us on the radio. We told people to keep an eye out for the car. When he came out, he was surrounded by 10 cops and a bunch of angry old guys pointing fingers and lecturing him.

We can take very little credit for it. It's the listeners. They're everything.

Emergencies

If there's a hurricane, earthquake, or other emergency, Perry & Price head to the studios.

Price: We couldn't get phone calls the last time there was an earthquake. We felt the earthquake and both headed to the radio station.

Perry: We had this poor kid at the studio Sunday morning who did everything right and got us back on the air.

Price: Fourteen straight hours is the longest we have been in the studio during an emergency. We cancel all the commercials — they want us to cancel, and then we try to make it up to the advertisers in the rest of the month.

Perry: If there's an emergency, then that's when we can actually do a job people care about. All we're trying to do is put people's fears to rest. Don't panic, no, no that's not true. It's going to be ok, we tell people.

Price: We're information brokers. Here's where you can go if you need help, just take it easy.

What was it like to work with Aku?

Perry: Aku really created the genre here of taking calls on air. He asked the engineer one day to put the phone on the radio. It had just never been done before. The engineer went 'how am I supposed to do that?'

Price: I was his replacement if he got sick or had to go someplace. When I first went down there and he was teaching me how to do the show, I was absolutely scared to death about the kind of responsibility that's involved with taking calls, going on the air and making snap judgments. Nobody really understands how great and masterful he was on the radio.

Perry: Aku had a perfect voice for AM radio. He just had the right timber and register. He was a musician. He understood sound, and how music and voice fit together.

Price: And he understood controversy. He knew how to piss people off. He was totally uninhibited too, unabashed, that's one of the qualities Mike has. He has his anal canal checked and he's talking about it on the radio the next day. I couldn't believe it. I could never do that. That's why we get along so well — because we're total opposites.

Perry: One of the things that made Aku so great is that he failed at everything else he did. He tried to be a concert violinist, comedian, television guy, and failed. When he put it all together for radio, it clicked. It worked. It was all perfect training for one thing — radio.

Price: I'm surprised no one has written a book about Aku.

Perry: There would be a dark side to that book. It would be a scary story. The truth is, he was lonely, and didn't have any friends, just a bunch of acquaintances at Waialae Country Club.

Price: Aku used to take me out at night and train me. He called me "Kid" all the time. For a former football coach to be called Kid by a failed violinist, it used to piss me off. He'd say "Kid, you're going with me to the Kahala tonight."

He'd have this beautiful girl on his arm, and we'd go down to the Maile Room, and he'd try to teach me to behave in public. We'd go out once a week. Kind of like a class. He'd say, "act like you own the place."

The other thing he told me. Never go on time. He'd take me out with him. He'd say "meet me at seven o'clock." I'd be there at a quarter to seven. He'd say, "if I tell you seven, that means we're going to walk in around twenty after, so that they're all looking for us."

I said, if I come in 20 minutes late, I'm going to crawl in. He said, "kid, don't look at the ground. Look up."

46

Does that mean he was also late to work?

Perry: Yes. We had him on tape, for just those occasions, saying things like "good morning ... a little ray of sunshine ... Aku here." His news guy, Bruce Jones, would do the news, and play pre-recorded little things Aku would say, and then cut to music or news, until Aku showed up.

Price: He'd call me up at 4:30 in the morning sometimes, when he's supposed to go on the air at five and say 'kid — I can't make it today."

I said, why didn't you call me earlier?

"Shut up," he'd say, "and get your ass in there!"

Aku used to tell me it's a slapstick business. "Don't be subtle. Price you're too subtle. Subtlety and sarcasm are not appreciated in this business. You've got to hit them like a pie in the face. That's radio. Don't be subtle. They won't get it. Just hit them right in the face with it."

I'd come in at 10 PM sometimes to prepare and he'd be there listening to classical music, prepping for the next day's show.

Perry: He'd be trying to figure out what to do to improve his show. And it always came down to some piece of classical music he thought he could play that would make the show better. People were listening for *him*. They didn't give a rip what he played. He could have played Vietnamese chants and they wouldn't have cared. He didn't know that. He thought it was the music.

"Aku used to call me "Kid" all the time," Larry Price recalls "For a former football coach to be called Kid by a failed violinist, used to piss me off." Honolulu Advertiser *photo.*

Cec Heftel covered many of Aku's gambling debts when he died in 1983. Honolulu Advertiser *photo.*

Price: When he died, the producer called me up and said Aku passed away. You have to tell the listeners. He left a letter we want you to read. We're not going to play any commercials. All we're going to do it take calls from listeners. It was a public eulogy of people calling.

We did that for three days, 5 hours a day. People wanted to say how much they loved and missed him, that they should build a bronze statue or monument to him, or have an Aku golf tournament, or that no one is ever going to take his place.

Women would call crying on the phone, sobbing, asking "what are we going to do?" He was actually a part of their lives, a part of their subconscious. I never had the impression that he was loved like that.

Aku used to gamble. When he passed away we took at least 25 calls from people he owed money to playing gin rummy, who wanted to know if Heftel would make good on it.

Perry: Cec took care of his formal debts with the big guys in Vegas and financial institutions, but not his little stuff.

Tragically flawed

Perry: Usually the tragic flaw is what makes you great. The really great people out there have tragic flaws. The people at the top of their profession, like Johnny Carson or Frank Sinatra, they do have tragic flaws. It's possible to be successful and do OK, but the people who really, really make a dent, usually have a tragic flaw.

Price: I think Aku's flaw was that he used himself as a standard for judging other people, not knowing how far he deviated from the norm. He thought the way he saw things was the way it was. It was amazing to me that he could be so smart and clever and not see that.

Perry: He was unable to run his personal life. He was the highest-paid DJ in the world, but spent 15% more than he earned.

Lawsuits

Perry: Aku would often say something incredibly slanderous and Cec was sued dozens of times. Once, Aku accused Henry Peters of paying off a cop who had pulled him over. And Cec would go, "oh s---," because every time he said something like that it cost him $20,000 to settle the lawsuit and avoid having to go to court.

Price: Aku told me, "they judge your greatness by how many lawsuits you get."

Perry: No, they don't.

Price: Cec got real tired of it, so he hired Dennis Sakaguchi to listen and bleep him if he said anything slanderous. He told the engineers he wanted whatever he said to be delayed 10 seconds before going out over the air.

Perry: The engineers created this Rube Goldberg device with 12-inch reels and tape running all over the room. Things started over here, and looped around, to other 12-inch reels and end up in this tape head over here. Dennis sat in this little room and listened and could push a button and silence something slanderous.

When I went to work there, I thought it was the funniest thing I'd ever seen. We've been here 24 years and never been sued. We have opinions on almost everything, but none are slanderous.

What 'American Princess' met her husband in Honolulu?

Left: Shirley Temple was the top actress when she arrived in Hawaii in 1935. She was just 7 years old. Above: Temple met her husband to be, Charles Black, at a party in Hawaii on her third trip here Honolulu Advertiser *photos.*

IT WAS LOVE AT FIRST SIGHT, for 22-year-old Shirley Temple, who met Hawaiian Pine executive Charles Black at a party in Honolulu in 1950. "I fell in love with him at first sight," Shirley said. "It sounds corny, but that's what happened. But I don't think he did with me."

Black had not seen any of her films and did not recognize her. "We were introduced," the former child star recalled, "and he said 'What do you do, are you a secretary?' I said, 'I can't even type. I make films.' It was very refreshing to me — a handsome guy who wasn't interested in Hollywood or anything about it."

Shirley Temple was separated at the time from her first husband, Jack Agar. She and her new beau spent a lot of time touring Oahu,

It was love at first sight, for Shirley. Hawaiian Pine exec. Charles Black almost skipped the party to go surfing.

Alfred Apaka sings with Shirley on KGU.

and going for swims. A friend, FBI director J. Edgar Hoover, ran a background check on him and found he had been a naval intelligence officer during World War II and had been awarded a Silver Star. They married later that year and spent 55 years together until Charles died in 2002.

The most famous child star in history came to the islands many times, the first in 1935 in the midst of the Great Depression. She stayed at the Royal Hawaiian, which created a drink made with Ginger Ale, grenadine syrup, orange juice, a maraschino cherry and a slice of lemon. They called it a *Shirley Temple*.

Temple broke into movies in *Stand Up and Cheer* in 1934 at the age of five. She performed in several more films that year, including *Bright Eyes*, where she first sang *On the Good Ship Lollipop*.

She was the top box office star in America when she first visited Hawaii in 1935.

When Shirley Temple arrived in Hawaii for the first time in 1935, 15,000 people greeted her ship at Aloha Tower. She was frightened by the crowd until she spotted Duke Kahanamoku. She yelled out to him, and minutes later was on his shoulders. Bishop Museum photo.

53

Which comedian's joke became a local company name?

Mahalo Airlines took its name from a Rap Reiplinger comedy routine. Honolulu Advertiser *photos.*

ERE'S A HINT: It was an airline. The joke was that they had four emergency exits — two in the front of the cockpit, and two in the rear of the cockpit. Party balloons could be used as flotation devices "should we run out of luck ... and plummet headlong into the raging surf below."

Companies are often named for the owner or their family. Sometimes where they are located becomes part of their name. Many were named for songs or movies. A few were named for alcoholic beverages, but Mahalo Airlines is the only one we've seen named after a comedian's skit. The comedian was Rap Reiplinger.

James Kawika Piimauna "Rap" Reiplinger was born in San Francisco in 1950 and adopted by a Hawaiian family made up mostly of cops and musicians. He studied acting at Punahou and hooked up with Ed Kaahea and James Grant Benton to form Booga Booga.

The satirical trio burst onto the comedy scene in the early 1970s at the Territorial Tavern on Bishop and Nimitz Highway. They took comedy to a new level, although it was totally rooted in everyday local experiences. Wayne Harada described it as "moke humor — da

Hawaii's greatest comedy team, Booga Booga was Rap Reiplinger, left, James Grant Benton, and Ed Ka'ahea.

kine real hang-loose, no-holds-barred, tell-it-like-it-is, earthy-vivid blalah comedy."

They seemed to be improvisational but it was actually ingeniously structured and rehearsed. One routine had Kaahea and Benton playing a couple of lolo's from Lanai trying to steal the King Kamehameha statue, played by Reiplinger, who managed to hold his pose even as they carried him away.

Rap left Booga Booga in 1977 because he felt he was stagnating. Andy Bumatai replaced him. Rap took off for L.A. and while the rain, freaks, geeks and nerds he met there made him homesick, they also inspired him to write the material for his first album — *Poi Dog with Crabs*.

Mountain Apple's Jon de Mello suggested he release the album and open a show at the Ala Moana Hotel simultaneously. It was a good call. Opening night was gangbusters.

Poi Dog featured several memorable comedy routines: *Mahalo Airlines* (flight 512 to Wailuku, Hana and Denver), *Room Service* (where the lolo hotel operator has trouble taking an order for a cheeseburger, fries and chocolate malt), and *Fate Yanagi* (a simple love song about surfing at Point Panic: "Tell Fate Yanagi I love her")

He created the soap opera *Young Kanakas* that contained a commercial for their sponsor, Wendell's:

Come we go to Wendell's
For one hell of a kaukau
It's a foot long laulau
Better than poi, better than pig
Wendell's laulau's frickin' big.

In *Pull Over*, Rap plays a driver stopped for traveling 95 mph in a 10 mph zone by an Officer Medeiros. His quick talking gets him out of the ticket.

Driver: Medeiros ... Medeiros ... not the Medeiros I thinking ... Eh! You're Auntie Nellie's brother's cousin George's nephew's son, eh?

Patrolman: Ahhhh, yeah, I t'ink so. How you know?

Driver: Cuz, uncle's bruddah's niece's Debra's husband, Dick, is my first cousin on my second mother's side!

Patrolman: Nnnnnnot!

Driver: We related!

Patrolman: Nnnnnnot!

Driver: We cousins!

Patrolman: Nnnnnnot!
Driver: Through Auntie Nellie!
Patrolman: Nnnnnnot!
Driver: In fact, I was on my way to see her.
Patrolman: Nnnnnnot!
Driver: Yeah, eh ... I late!
Patrolman: Nnnnnnot!
Driver: I gotta get going. I see you laters. B'bye!

Reiplinger wrote and starred in a TV comedy special called *Rap's Hawaii* that was first broadcast in 1982 on KGMB. It won Rap an Emmy Award.

Rap decided to create a comedy group in 1981 that he would write for and direct. He hired four men and four women and called the group Hats. Hawaii's top public relations person, Kitty Lagareta was a young mother of two at the time, decided to audition, and was hired.

"It was surreal for me to actually be working with him," Lagareta says. "Rap was a great comedian. He was a friendly, low-key, calm, funny guy."

"He took us to J.C. Penney's at Ala Moana and he personally picked out identical T-shirts and tight Jordache jeans for us. He had the sales ladies running around, and he was ringmaster. It was a comedy routine in and of itself."

"He told us he was going to pay. We got to the counter, and it was $330. The lady said, sorry sir, your credit card doesn't work. He gave her another card, also no good. We all ended up having to buy our own."

Rap acted as the creative director and manager, but did not perform with them. "He wrote some of our skits, but we all had to write our own as well," Lagareta recalls. "He encouraged us to look for the hilarious side of everyday stuff. It was taking a common situation and twisting it a little. What if it was this wacky or this crazy? That's what he enjoyed the most."

"I got the feeling Rap didn't work that hard to be funny. It was like wearing a different set of glasses. Things just looked differently. He was so creative."

One of Lagareta's monologues was called by Wayne Harada as an "exercise of astonishing wit." From then on, Rap teased Kitty about it, calling her "the astonishing wit."

"We performed at the Comedy Corner to many packed houses. I loved the group so much. It was such great fun to do it. Nothing we did was bad, although some routines were funnier than others."

Lagareta thinks Rap created the group so he didn't have to be on all the time. "It was a source of revenue for him. He paid us $30 a show and kept the rest. This ended up being our downfall. After awhile, we performed more but got less. We suspected he had a drug problem. At some point we didn't get paid at all. The group fell apart and I never saw him after that."

"Rap was dynamic and funny, but then would get serious, contemplative and sort of dark. That's where some of his humor came from. We saw more of that dark side as time went on."

Rap was found along a Maunawili trail in 1984, dead from a drug overdose. He may be gone, but he blazed across Hawaii's skies and left a wake of amazing comedy routines that thousands still smile about to this day.

Who was Hawaii's first Japanese visitor in 1844?

"John" Manjiro was the first person from Japan to come to Hawaii in 1844.

THE FIRST PERSON from Japan to come to Hawaii was Manjiro Nakahama. Manjiro was a 14-year old fisherman who was shipwrecked on a small, deserted island in a storm in 1841 with four others. A U.S. whaler picked them up six months later, but could not take them back to Japan because it was forbidden.

The fishermen stayed in Honolulu, but Manjiro decided to travel to Massachusetts with Captain William Whitfield. "John," as he was called, stayed with the Whitfield family and became the top student at school.

When the California Gold Rush began, John joined and earned enough money to buy a boat. He returned to Japan to see his mother, but was soon jailed for leaving and returning to Japan.

When Commodore Perry sailed into Yokohama Bay in 1853, Manjiro was called to advise and translate. He told the Shogun that "America greatly hopes to enjoy a deep and abiding friendship with Japan. America does not come with suspicious designs but with a full and open heart." President Coolidge called Manjiro "America's first ambassador to Japan."

In 1881, 37 years after Manjiro's arrival, King Kalakaua became the first person from Hawaii to visit Japan.

How an Aiea girl became the 'Divine Miss M'

RUTH MIDLER NAMED HER BABY, born on December 1, 1945, after one of her favorite actresses – Bette Davis. The Aiea native graduated from Radford High School and went on to study acting at the University of Hawaii. In 1965, Bette landed a bit part in the movie *Hawaii*.

She had to travel to Los Angeles to film one scene and later decided to pursue acting in New York. In 1967, Bette landed the roles of Tzeitel, the eldest daughter in *Fiddler on the Roof*. She appeared a few times on TV talk shows and worked as a go-go dancer at a bar on Broadway while she continued her acting, dancing and singing lessons.

By chance, Bette heard that the owner of a gay club, the Continental Baths, was looking for a weekend entertainer. The pay was $50 a night. Eddie Sherman described her like a "wild, young Carmen Miranda with a touch of Mae West." She dazzled her

audience with hits from the 1930s through the 1960s. Her accompanist was a young man named Barry Manilow.

Manilow said he never felt such electricity in a performance. "I found myself laughing hysterically at her jokes, weeping at her ballads, and at the end I was on my feet like everybody else, cheering for her. I had never seen

Aiea girl, Bette Midler was named for Bette Davis.
Honolulu Advertiser *photos.*

60

Bette's big break came when she was hired to entertain at a New York gay bath house, where she dazzled audiences .

anything like it." Bette had become the Divine Miss M.

Johnny Carson made her a semi-regular on the *Tonight Show*. Atlantic Records released her first album in 1972 called, *The Divine Miss M*. The album sold over 100,000 records during its first month, and included the hit *Boogie Woogie Bugle Boy*.

Bette was nominated for an Academy Award for her first film, *The Rose* (1979), and she won two Golden Globes for her performance. Her 1980 album, *Divine Madness*, went platinum. Bette also published *A View from a Broad,* of humorous vignettes from her first world tour.

Bette's films included *Down and Out in Beverly Hills*, *Ruthless People*, (1986); *Outrageous Fortune* (1987); and *Big Business* and *Beaches* (1988). The soundtrack of *Beaches* contained the number one single, *Wind Beneath my Wings*, which won a Grammy. In 1991, she won a second Grammy for the hit *From a Distance*.

When Johnny Carson retired from the *Tonight Show* in 1992, it was Bette, who sang the emotional last song, *One for my baby and one for the Road*, a fitting finale for the King of Late Night.

Ah, the Ala Wai

Here's what the Ala Wai Canal might have looked like if it continued to the ocean near the Natatorium. Honolulu Advertiser *photos.*

MANY OF US KNOW THE ALA WAI CANAL was built in 1926 to drain the swamps of Waikiki, but did you know that the original proposal called for it to continue through Kapiolani Park and meet the sea near the Natatorium? Or that it was once suggested to extend Ewa to Pearl Harbor as a rapid transit system?

The idea for the Ala Wai Canal was the vision of one man, Lucius Pinkham, president of the Territorial Board of Health. In 1906, Pinkham proposed a Waikiki Canal, "as lovely as the canals in Venice," which would divert the Makiki, Manoa, and Palolo streams that fed the marshlands, duck ponds and rice paddies of Waikiki.

Pinkham saw the tourism potential of Waikiki, which numbered fewer than 2,000 visitors annually back then. When he became the Territorial Governor in 1913 the project got underway. It was completed in 1926.

Lucius Pinkham

The original idea was for the canal to continue through Kapiolani Park to the ocean near the Natatorium, making Waikiki a true island. A low-lying area of the park that regularly flooded would become a recreational lake.

Concerns were raised that four bridges would have to be built, and that trash and silt could wash up on Waikiki beaches.

In 1967, the Rotary Club of Waikiki resurrected the idea as a solution to the polluted waters of the Ala Wai.

City planners raised the same concerns that were mentioned 35 years earlier. Additionally, the canal would have to go through either the Kapahulu Library or Jefferson Elementary.

One of the most bizarre suggestions for the Ala Wai Canal was made in 1965 to extend the canal through Ala Moana Beach Park and on to Pearl Harbor! Hydrofoils would pick up passengers at Ala Moana Center, downtown, Honolulu Airport, and major interchanges. The proposal went nowhere.

In the last 100 years, Waikiki has evolved from an "unsightly, unsanitary marshland of doubtful soggy value," with more ducks than people, into a worldwide tourist attraction that generates over $10 billion annually. The cause of that change has been the Ala Wai Canal, and as such, its value is immeasurable.

It might be polluted, but it's undoubtedly the most important engineering accomplishment in the state.

An Unintentional Pioneer

"I've never set a goal in my life," Coble says. Honolulu Advertiser *photos.*

LINDA COBLE is an enigma. She's been a pioneer—the first woman in many arenas — but never by design. "I've never set a goal in my life," she says. "I think I am more a believer in fate, and that if you consistently apply yourself and work hard, you can rise above life's unpredictability. In the face of professional and personal challenges, flexibility is key. I've avoided rigid goals."

Coble was the first woman to earn a broadcast journalism scholarship to the University of Oregon. She landed a job in the newsroom at KHVH-TV, and was Hawaii's first female reporter. Two years later, they promoted her to Hawaii's first female anchor. She also was among the first female members of the Rotary Club of Honolulu, its first female president, and Hawaii Rotary's first female Governor.

It wasn't necessarily easy, Coble says. "I knocked on doors at TV stations throughout Oregon when I was getting close to graduating from the University of Oregon. The personnel director at KOIN Channel 6 told me to return after I had more experience and 'a sex change operation.' I was crushed. A dozen years later, when KOIN hired me as the affiliate's first female anchor, I found that same personnel director and in my deepest voice said 'I'm baaaaack.'"

Coble's first job in Hawaii was at KHVH – Ch. 4 as a newsroom secretary in 1969. "I answered phones, took suits to cleaners, swept the floor, and earned $1.50 an hour. But I watched over the shoulder of everybody, and learned what they were doing."

There was a car bombing at Holiday Mart one day and Coble was the only one in the newsroom. "They looked around, and all the reporters were gone. So they sent me," Coble continues. "They knew I had the skills. I had studied and shadowed reporters."

The producers liked what she did and she was made a reporter.

Two years later, in 1971, Coble was anchoring the news at KHVH (now KITV). "They decided to call us the 'Foxiest Team in Town.' They made a glass coffee table set, and suggested I cross my legs a couple of times during the newscast."

"I didn't comprehend that it might be unusual for this chick from Oregon to be telling locals the news of the day. I couldn't pronounce Kalakaua. If something was happening in Ewa, I turned and asked on air, where was that?"

One of Coble's biggest scoops involved the late Senator Barry Goldwater of Arizona. "Barry Goldwater was a buddy of my dad's in the Air Force. One evening Don Rockwell gave me the assignment to interview Goldwater on his way home from

Coble was promoted from newsroom secretary in 1969 to reporter when there was a car bombing at Holiday Mart and she was the only one in the newsroom. "So they sent me," Coble says.

65

Sen. Barry Goldwater gave Coble her first big scoop.

Cambodia. His plane stopped to refuel here and Rockwell thought I could catch a shot of the plane refueling."

"My cameraman and I showed up at Hickam AFB and we could see the plane across the tarmac. I asked a man in a uniform to tell Barry Goldwater that Linda Coble was here to see him. My cameraman and the guy in uniform looked at me like I was an idiot. But he walked across the tarmac, and spoke to the senator."

"I could see him look in my direction for a moment, and then he waved for me to join him." Coble ran across the tarmac. Goldwater greeted her — "Linda, how the hell is Bob?" — "my dad. We had a great conversation about his trip and the war in Vietnam."

"We should have nuked them," Goldwater said, referring to the North Vietnamese. The suggestion we seriously consider using nuclear weapons in South East Asia made huge headlines across the country, Coble recounts. "You heard it first on KITV. It was early in my career, one of my first reports, and it was a huge scoop."

KGMB

In 1972, Cec Heftel hired Coble to join KGMB's news team with Bob Sevey, Tim Tindle, Bob Jones, and Joe Moore on sports. "Cec knew the value of everyone in that room and paid them accordingly. He gave main anchors ratings points as an incentive. He understood that to keep a team together was important. Cec Heftel cared about me. He knew I would never let him down."

Bob Sevey

"Bob Sevey was our mentor, our guru, our quality control expert. He assigned 'beats'. Bambi Weil covered Government. Someone else had the Education beat. I was on the Cops beat for a long time, working with Police Chief Keala, beat officers, and organized crime figures, who amazingly would often call me with tips. It was exciting."

"Sevey told me to pretend I was talking to one person when I looked in the camera lens — your grandmother or whomever you want, when you do the news that day. It was wonderful advice."

KGMB's 1987 lineup included Bob Jones, Coble and Larry Beil.

"Sevey was a true role model for all of us. We learned to cop to our mistakes, report fairly and objectively, and keep our personal biases out of our stories."

Joe Moore

"Joe Moore was notorious for trying to scare me. One time there was a circus in town. He had the trainer bring an 8-foot tall bear into the newsroom in chains while I was on the air. It came up behind me, and even lurched for me! Joe loved it!"

One of Moore's best on-air tricks was his Evel Knievel impersonation. Knievel was a motorcycle daredevil. "Joe found a tricycle and fog maker amongst some props from the *Checkers & Pogo* show. He rode the tricycle from the sports desk over a gap to the anchor desk, ala Evel Knievel, and crashed off camera. A second later, he appeared wearing a burned T-shirt. It was hilarious. He must have spent all day preparing for it."

"There was always something funny going on," Coble continues. "People loved it. That's why they tuned in. Some viewers would go to sleep at 9 PM but set their clocks for 10 PM to catch the news. We killed back then. We had a 60 share. That's three times what anybody has now. It was huge."

"Bob Jones would occasionally strip down during the newscast just to unravel me. He would be sitting there in the anchor chair, taking his pants off, while the camera was on someone else. The audience couldn't see behind the desk. I had to keep a straight face."

"Boxers or briefs," we ask? "Boxers."

Mr. Linda Coble

When her stepfather died in 1981, Linda moved back to Oregon to live with her mom, landing a job as the first female co-anchor at

KOIN-TV. The newsman filling the anchor seat until her arrival was Kirk Matthews. "There was a party for January birthdays at the station and we learned we were both born on the same day — same year, January 10, 1947."

Matthews' morning news crew did a week of shows in Honolulu. "He really got Hawaii. It was love at first sight. Some people get off the plane and inhale the aroma, and they immediately fit in. It sticks to their bones. It happened to Kirk. I knew if our relationship grew, and I wanted to go home to Hawaii, he would come willingly and would fit right in."

In 1983, homesickness drew Coble back to the islands and the job Bob Sevey had been holding for her. Matthews soon followed. "It was a professional risk. He called it jumping off the Pali." They married in 1984, and by then Kirk was the KGMB night beat reporter. He had to put up with being called "Mr. Linda Coble," until he was offered the hosting job for $9,000 *Jackpot Bingo*, which lasted eleven months. "We couldn't walk down the street without someone yelling out 'heh, Kirk, call my number'. So much for 'heh, Linda, take my picture.'"

All in the Ohana

The local comedy classic, *All in the Ohana*, aired in 1980 and Coble was in it. "People still say to this day, 'Eh, you da one, on dat Andy Bumatai.' So I respond

"We've got to compress the information we gather under deadline into an appealing, engaging, visual, factual story that grabs the viewer," Coble says.

with a line 'Tutu' said: "In da morning, when you wake up, your hair stay curly li dat?"

"*All in the Ohana* was filmed in a little house in Waimanalo. I played a reporter and interviewed the family. I recall wearing a navy blue jacket and blue tube top - ha!" Coble exclaims. "Andy Bumatai played all five members of the family and spent hours in the make-up chair."

"Andy was gracious. He knew what he was doing and never skipped a beat juggling all those roles. He was never uptight. When I goofed up, like forgetting to hemo my shoes at the door, he just shrugged, ad libbed a joke, and left it in."

"I got so many wonderful comments on that after it aired. Maybe I was the only woman willing to make "A" and get away with it." "The ability to communicate under pressure is a must in television news. We're doing one to two minute stories. We've got to compress the information we gather under deadline into an appealing, engaging, visual, factual story that grabs the viewer. And do it with the appropriate expression on the face and in the voice. I am honored to have worked alongside some of the best."

"No longer delivering the news affords me the opportunity to advocate for the causes and address the concerns that always have dwelled within me. The prevention of child abuse and neglect, foster family issues, Kids Voting Hawaii, and all of the programs of Rotary fill my volunteer time, and my heart."

Kelli Abe Trifonovich worked with Coble at KGMB. She recalls Elisa Yadao describing Linda Coble's reporting style: "Look at how she puts stories together. It's like a gift."

What lullaby did Harry Owens write for his daughter?

ROYAL HAWAIIAN HOTEL BANDLEADER Harry Owens had a daughter born on October 19, 1934. Her name was Leilani. He was inspired to write *Sweet Leilani* for her as a lullaby. Owens says the "words and music flowed like a rippling stream. The actual composing and writing took only an hour and never has a note or word been changed."

However, one day in 1937, crooner Bing Crosby came to Hawaii to research an upcoming movie: *Waikiki Wedding*. He dined and danced at the Royal Hawaiian Hotel.

In his book, *Sweet Leilani: The Story Behind the Song* (1970, Hula House), Owens recalls Bing dancing up to Owens and asking, "'what's the name of the song?' *Sweet Leilani*," I told him. ... 'Can't pronounce it,' said Bing, and he danced away."

Inspired by the birth of his daughter, Leilani, in 1934, Harry Owens wrote Sweet Leilani in less than an hour. Bishop Museum photos.

"In 20 minutes, he was back at the bandstand. 'How about playing that song again, Harry? You know, the one I can't pronounce.' We played "*Sweet Leilani*" again. In fact, no less than five more times Bing requested the song he couldn't pronounce."

Songwriters Leo Robin and Ralph Rainger wrote the music for *Waikiki Wedding* and did not want to include *Sweet Leilani*, but Crosby insisted. He had good instincts. The song became Crosby's first of 22 gold records, and it spent half a year on the charts. *Sweet Leilani* won the 1937 Academy Award for Best Song of the Year.

Over 25 million copies of *Sweet Leilani* were sold, and some say it revived the recording industry during the Great Depression.

"Sweet Leilani, Heavenly Flower,
  nature fashioned roses kissed with dew,
  and then she placed them in a bower,
  it was the start of you.

Sweet Leilani, Heavenly Flower,
I dreamed of paradise for two;
you are my paradise completed,
you are my dream come true."

Owens and Leilani stroll in front of the Royal Hawaiian Hotel, where Bing Crosby heard the song. He sang it in the movie "Waikiki Wedding." It became his first gold record, and won an Academy Award.

Harry Owens composed over 300 songs including *Hawaii Calls*, *Hawaiian Paradise*, *The Cockeyed Mayor of Kaunakakai*, and *Princess Poo-poo-ly has Plenty Papaya*. Johnny Carson called him Mr. Hawaii.

The man who interned at an internment camp

YOU'VE PROBABLY HEARD OF HIGHWAY INN, the Hawaiian food restaurant in Waipahu. But did you know the founder learned the restaurant business in Arkansas and California internment camps during World War II?

Seiichi Toguchi was born in Hawaii in 1914, but when his father broke his leg and couldn't work, four year old Seiichi and two older sisters were sent to Okinawa. Grandparents and relatives raised them until Seiichi was 14 and returned to Hawaii. He went to work as a dishwasher at the old City Café, owned by the Hamamoto family, where he later learned how to cook.

Bobby Toguchi, far left, has recently passed the Highway Inn baton to daughter, Regina, center. Lending a hand are George and Gary Toguchi, top row, and Shirley (Toguchi) Higa (far right). Photo Courtesy: Tina Yuen, Pacific Business News.

When World War II broke out, Seiichi was interned because he was a kibei-nissei, (one raised in Japan), and was thus suspect. He, his wife Sachiko, and their three children were sent from California by train to Jerome, Arkansas. Later in 1944, the family was then transferred to Tulelake, California. Seiichi was assigned to work in the cafeteria. There he worked with other cooks from around the country, several of which had been executive chefs at top restaurants.

"His internment was free schooling for him," says granddaughter Regina Toguchi. "It was a catalyst, and gave him a foundation for running a restaurant when the war was over."

Mr. Toguchi came up with the idea of opening a restaurant to support his growing family, now with seven children. His mother-in-law, Masa Asato, went from house to house and borrowed $3,000 for him to start Highway Inn in Waipahu in 1947. Seiichi

Seiichi Toguchi, far right, learned to cook at World War II Internment camps. He opened Highway Inn, sixty years ago, when he returned to Hawaii.

named it for Farrington Highway, on which it was located. It was on historic Depot Road where the Bank of Hawaii and Mid-Town Radio are now.

Street widening forced them to move up the street in the 1960s, below the old sugar mill, about where the former Big Way Super-market and Arakawa's store was.

Bobby Toguchi recalls his father sitting on a cushion on a bucket to rest. "We used to have on old cash register that would make a 'ka-ching' sound when orders were rung up. Dad was so attentive and aware of what was happening around him that, although he was responsible for making all the orders, he still listened to the 'ka-chings' and could tell if they missed one. Ka-ching, ka-ching, ka-ching … 'one more,' he'd say … ka-ching." "He cooked the meals, and could still keep an ear open to make sure the waitress rung them all up," Regina says.

In 1979, Seiichi wanted to retire and convinced his son Bobby to leave Japan Airlines and take over. "It was either that or close," Bobby says. "He worked so hard to make it go. He wanted it to

The Toguchi's were sent to Arkansas and California Internment camps during World War II.

continue." Bobby moved it to its present site, on Leoku Street in 1984.

Bobby also expanded, opening the Highway Inn Seafood Market in 2000 next to the restaurant. Highway Inn Seafood Market serves a variety of fresh fish, assorted poke and fresh produce.

He also added a Highway Inn Catering Service for all occasions — baby luaus, graduations, birthdays, weddings, baby showers, retirements, business functions, and funerals.

Bobby had a stroke in 2003 and his daughter, Regina, felt compelled to take over the restaurant. "I felt an obligation to the family and customers," she says. "It was almost the same circumstances as with my father and his father."

"This is an old style Hawaiian hole-in-the-wall," Regina says. "Many of our employees have worked here 15-20 years. People get a hello and a kiss on the cheek here. It's a comfortable place where we know many customers by name. Many invite us to birthday parties and weddings."

"We're like a gathering place. Lots of customers run into old friends here and it isn't uncommon for one table to pay the check of another. I've never seen that anywhere else. It seems to happen all the time."

"Some bring their mainland friends, who tell us Highway Inn is like going back in time to a Hawaii that existed 50 years ago."

"Others sneak in here by themselves and ask us not to tell their family or friends they were here, when they come in together. It's odd. Almost like a guilty pleasure. Maybe they think they'd be upset they didn't bring them, or take home stew and pipikaula for them."

So next time you're in Waipahu, stop in. Maybe you'll run into old friends, and if you're lucky, maybe someone else will pay your bill.

Who was the 'King of Pidgin'?

Lippy Espinda was the King of Pidgin. He popularized the use of the word "Skaka." Honolulu Advertiser *photos.*

THE FIRST PERSON to use pidgin in advertising seems to be Chotaru Miyamoto who founded Musashiya in 1896. Residents were so delighted with his newspaper ads, that began running in 1920, that they sent them to friends all over the world.

David Akana Espinda Jr., owned a used car lot and gas station on Kalakaua Avenue around 1960. He wanted a unique TV commercial. "I used pidgin and it caught on like wildfire," said Lippy, as he was known to his friends.

At the end, he'd say "shaka brah!" This became his signature.

"It was a word we used as kids playing marbles." Espinda explained. It came to mean "anything fine."

School teachers complained, but the public loved it. He became known as the King of Pidgin. KHON gave him his own TV show — *Lippy's Lanai Theatre*, and he had regular appearances on *Hawaii Five-0*, minus the pidgin.

Many thought he was Portuguese, but he was Hawaiian, Chinese, Spanish and Irish. "My mother's name was Molly Ryan. I let you in on a secret. I might be related to Jack Lord. His real name is Jack Ryan. When I told him dat, he said 'heaven forbid!'"

Lippy passed away in 1975, but his "shaka brah" has become part of island vocabulary.

Who predicted in 1923 that the Japanese would attack Pearl Harbor?

Billy Mitchell predicted a surprise Japanese attack on Pearl Harbor in 1923 – 18 years before it happened.

ARMY MAJ. GEN. Billy Mitchell was the first person to predict a Japanese attack on Pearl Harbor.

Even more amazing, he did it in 1923, before aircraft carriers! How could they do it? Mitchell suggested 100 Japanese planes could fly to Midway island and be refueled by submarines.

They would then fly to Niihau, refuel and attack on a Sunday morning at 7:30 AM. There were no radios on Niihau back then.

He was able to convince the Robinson Family to plow Niihau island's flat areas to prevent its use as an airfield, at their own cost. Fifty square miles was crisscrossed with the furrows. It took three men and eight years to do it.

Billy Mitchell died in 1935, and never learned that he was wrong. The Japanese attacked at 7:55 AM … not 7:30.

In 1942, he was posthumously promoted to Major General. In 1946, he was awarded a Congressional Medal of Honor. Mitchell had pushed for an independent Air Force after World War I. It was finally created on September 18, 1947.

The War Department buried his report and its far-fetched predictions, but finally declassified and made them public in 1958.

"Prophecy & Honor"

Joe Moore portrayed Col. Billy Mitchell in "Prophecy & Honor."

I N AUGUST 2007, Joe Moore produced a play at the Hawaii Theatre about the court martial of Billy Mitchell, called *Prophecy & Honor*. The production raised $40,000 for the Pacific Aviation Museum at Ford Island.

It took Joe two years to track down the trial transcripts. "The more I read about Mitchell, the more he reminded me of my father — a very professional, very stubborn but very sharp, dedicated, career officer who didn't back down from his superiors when he felt he was right. It cost Billy Mitchell, and it cost my dad. So there was that appeal of it relating to my father."

"Mitchell was so ahead of his time in assessing what air power could mean for the country and he didn't understand how the top brass in the Army and Navy didn't get it."

Moore decided to produce the play and was able to get Richard Dreyfuss and George Segal on board. "Once the agents got it to them - bingo they were on."

"Billy Mitchell was asked if he was going to live to see his predictions come true," Moore continues "and he said 'I just wish I could be there for the big show' — meaning the next war — 'because you're really going to see what air power can do.'"

Col Billy Mitchell predicted in 1923 that the Japanese would use flat areas of Niihau to launch an attack on Pearl Harbor. This is an actual tractor the Robinson Family used to cut furrows in the ground to prevent planes from landing there. It's on loan to the Pacific Aviation Museum on Ford Island.

How did Dayna Johnson become Sweetie Pacarro?

SWEETIE PACARRO WAS BORN DAYNA LYNN Pacarro and all her friends called her "D" growing up. "When I became the producer for the KSSK Saturday Perry & Price Show at the Hanohano Room in the summer of 1990, Larry Price told me I couldn't use Dayna Johnson," Pacarro recalls.

"It was too boring, Larry said, for radio. It was too plain. From Day One, Larry never used my married name, Johnson, and rarely called me Dayna. He always called me 'Pacarro.' 'Hey Pacarro. Get me the sports page. Pacarro — come in here for a second.'"

"You know, Larry, I told him, I am a Johnson. And he said, 'you're a Pacarro; you look like a Pacarro, you act like a Pacarro, you're a Pacarro. That's going to be your name. We're going to find a name for you,' he told me, 'and it's going to be Pacarro. And that was it."

Larry Price gave Dayna Johnson the name "Sweetie Pacarro."

"'You always smell so sweet,' he said one day. 'You have a sweet personality. That's it! Sweetie Pacarro!' A lot of people think it's my given name, but it was Larry Price who gave me the name. That was the best name they could pick. I love it."

"It was hard at first for my

high school friends, but they got used to it. I joke with my husband, are you sure you don't want to change your name to Pacarro? 'No,' he says. It's a big joke with us. And when people call him Mr. Pacarro, it's hilarious. He goes with it and never says that he's not."

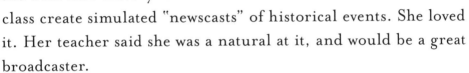

Breaking into broadcasting

Sweetie became interested in broadcasting in her freshman year at Star of the Sea. Her history teacher made the class create simulated "newscasts" of historical events. She loved it. Her teacher said she was a natural at it, and would be a great broadcaster.

She studied broadcast journalism at Chaminade, and Nestor Garcia, a distant relative, got her an internship at KHON2. "I thought I'd be the next Joe Moore," Sweetie says. When she passed him in the hall, she told him she wanted his job someday. "You can have it," was Joe's teasing response.

When she graduated, Nestor called again with a real job – KSSK was hiring. "Linda Coble interviewed me to be her news assistant and hired me in January 1990."

"Linda was fabulous, but I used to drive her crazy. I'd be in at five in the morning and I'd come in so happy. I'd be singing along to the music and dancing. I had all this energy to burn. I don't need any caffeine. It irritated her. She told me to run around the building a couple of times."

"Perry and Price, God bless them, welcomed me into their arms. Linda Coble got me in, she trained me, she got me into the news area and Perry and Price took me over for their show."

In the summer of 1990, Sweetie started helping them at their Saturday morning show at the Hanohano Room as the location producer. "I would coordinate all the guests, get them to their seats, and onto the stage when it was time. I interacted with the audience, and told Perry and Price who was in the room that would be interesting to talk to on air."

Psychically looking deep into your da kine

One frequent feature at Saturday's show is having Larry Price, the Portuguese Psychic, predict the sex of your unborn child.

"We put a turban on Larry's head while Mike tells the audience that 'eons ago, in the great Kakaako desert, Larry was riding his camel, Achmed Madeiros.' He will now predict the sex of your unborn child. How can he do this? By psychically looking deep into your da kine."

Larry examines the woman and asks her to show him her hands. "If they put palms up, Larry says it's a boy. If they're down, it's a girl.

"Perry & Price groomed me. They raised me and watched my family grow. It may not be by blood, but they are a part of my family."

If one is up and the other down, oh, oh — transvestite. Or maybe a quarterback. It's always hilarious."

Yuban

"At one time, one of our sponsors, Yuban needed a commercial, and someone wrote and sang one on Saturday. Y-U-B-A-N...Yuban! A few weeks later, someone else had written one and performed it. It got out of hand," Sweetie recalls. "We couldn't stop people from bringing their Yuban songs."

"Barbershoppers have done it.

Na Leo Pilimehana did it. When William Hung recorded *She Bangs*, someone used the music and substituted Yu-Ban, Yu-Ban for *She Bangs*. It's made Hawaii the top market in the country for Yuban coffee."

A match really made in heaven

Sweetie married her high school sweetheart, and believes they were "set up" by their grandfathers, who are buried, coincidentally, five graves away from each other at Hawaiian Memorial Park.

"After we dated about a year, Brad took me to put flowers on his grandfather's grave. I told him, my grandfather is buried here too. Turns out they were twenty-feet away from each other. They died about the same time. So Brad introduces me to his grandfather. I go up and introduce him to my grandfather. Is it destiny, or fate that they are buried so close to each other, or did they set us up? We think they were 'chatting' — 'my granddaughter would be perfect for your grandson' - and decided to get us together!"

Brad and Sweetie had another connection from beyond the grave. "His great, great grandparents are buried at a small cemetery on the street where I grew up. I used to play at their grave when I was a kid and take care of it. When Brad and I had our first date, he said he knew where I lived because his ancestors were buried there. I said, 'Samuel and Elizabeth Johnson!?' 'Yes, how do you know?' he asked. Oh my God, what an amazing coincidence. How did we not meet before, I wondered."

"KSSK is the greatest place to work," Sweetie says. "I love the people and they love me. It's a great environment. I love my job. I started working here when I was 21 years old. I was the youngest person. Perry and Price took care of me. They groomed me. They raised me and watched my family grow. It may not be by blood, but they are a part of my family."

Who was the King of Hawaiian Sweet Bread?

ROBERT TAIRA WAS THE NINTH OF ELEVEN children born to Okinawan immigrants who came to Hawaii in 1906 to work at the Kohala sugar plantation. Robert became a translator during World War II and saw that Japan would become a huge market for western goods after the war.

He came back to Hilo to study baking, but the Korean War kept him from returning to Japan. "A civilian couldn't get a permit to go to Japan," he explained. So, with $400 in loans, he opened Robert's Bakery in Hilo in 1950. He moved his bakery and coffee shop in 1963 to Honolulu, at 1936 So. King Street, near McCully. He later opened at Eaton Square and the Kaimuki Shopping Center.

In 1977, Taira opened a 30,000 square foot wholesale bakery, King's Hawaiian Bakery, in Torrance, California. He soon became the leading maker of sweet bread nationwide, and his company was grossing over $25 million annually. In 2003, they built a larger, 150,000 square foot facility in Los Angeles.

Robert Taira was a visionary, a local Horatio Alger. From a three-stool coffee shop in Hilo, he built an empire that employs over 300 people and sells its products in 50 major markets across the country. "My generation started from scratch," Taira said. "It's up to them (the next generation) to carry on. You have to be global-minded from here on. That's the reason why we went to the mainland."

His King Street coffee shop closed in 1993. It was a very sad day for many of his loyal customers. Taira died in 2003 and his son,

Mark is now CEO. "You always got to think about what the public wants, with reasonable prices and quality," Taira mused about the lessons he had learned. "Quality is first. You don't cheapen the price at the expense of quality. That's the key to success. Then the product sells itself."

Robert Taira took King's Bakery from Hilo to Honolulu and then global. Honolulu Advertiser *photo.*

Which event at Johnston Island was visible in Hawaii?

IN 1958, THE SKIES OF HAWAII WERE lit up on several occasions by nuclear tests at Johnston Island, 700 miles away.

The first explosion on August 1, 1958 was clearly visible around 1 AM in the Territory. The *Star-Bulletin* reported that "islanders who were up at that time saw a bright flash of light to the south-west, followed by a reddish fireball."

Even though Governor Quinn and military officials had warned us in advance of the test, the public greeted it with "a mild wave of panic," the papers reported.

A viewer 2500 miles south in Fiji reported seeing it, too. He described long streaks of lighting that seemed to flash downward from high in the sky. "Then a huge, round, reddish cloud appeared which burst after about 20 minutes into assorted colors which slowly spread outward."

When the second nuclear test occurred, islanders were better prepared, holding "Atomic Parties," with snacks and blankets at prime viewing locations.

How could we see such an event 700 miles away? The nuclear explosion took place 80 miles above the island. The top of the fireball was even higher than that. From 700 miles away, the curvature of the earth would prevent us from seeing anything at ground level. But we could see anything bright enough above 60 miles in height.

This was the first rocket-launched nuclear test by the United States. Its purpose was to measure the effects of high altitude nuclear explosions to be used in anti-ballistic missiles.

The 3.8-megaton warhead was 250 times more powerful than the bomb dropped on Hiroshima at the end of World War II.

On July 9, 1962, a 1.45-megaton bomb exploded at an altitude of 240 miles. An artificial aurora lasted seven minutes. The unforeseen electromagnetic pulse caused power-main surges on Oahu, knocked out streetlights, blew fuses and circuit breakers, and triggered burglar alarms. The explosion supercharged the Van Allen radiation belts, resulting in several satellites malfunctioning.

Hawaii held "Atomic Parties" to watch nuclear tests on Johnston Island in 1958. Honolulu Advertiser *photo.*

Which woman's middle name means 'heart of the sea?'

THIS WOMAN WAS THE FIRST FEMALE LIFEGUARD in the City and County of Honolulu in the late 1970s. She co-founded the Women's International Surfing Association in 1975. And she's affectionately known as the Queen of Makaha.

Yes, she was Rell Kapoliokaehukai Sunn. Kapoliokaehukai — means "Heart of the Sea."

Rell was born in Makaha in 1950 and lived her entire life there. Her Chinese, Hawaiian, Irish parents had 5 children. Rell's childhood was spent in and near the water, surfing from the young age of four, diving and paddling.

"Before I could read words, I could read the ocean, I could read the tides, the wind on the ocean,"Rell recalled. "I thought I knew everything I ever needed to know just from being on the beach."

Both men and women surfed before Captain Cook arrived. "It was a tradition for men and women to surf together," Sunn told the BBC. "When a woman would choose to ride a wave with a man, it was the precursor to them making love on the beach after."

"The traditional concept of surfing as a way to impress a potential mate was something that the Christian missionaries needed to quell in order to 'civilize' the Hawaiian people. The side effect, of course, was the death of women's surfing for the most part."

In the mid-1950s, the Makaha International Surfing Championships brought people from all over the world to the Leeward side. "There were these men, telling these great stories, and I swore

Rell Sunn, the Queen of Makaha. Honolulu Advertiser *photos.*

then that women could tell these same wonderful stories," Sunn told filmmakers Charlotte Lagarde and Lisa Denker, whose 1997 award-winning *Heart of the Sea*, documented her life.

Sunn was Hawaii's first female lifeguard. She helped launch the Women's Surfing Hui, the Women's Professional Surfing Association, the Women's Professional Surfing Tour, and the Menehune Surf Meet for children in 1975. For her efforts, she was dubbed the "Queen of Makaha."

Sunn battled breast cancer for 16 years, and passed away in January 1998 at the age of 47. Over 3,000 people came to Makaha for her funeral. Her ashes were scattered at sea, with water and sand friends had brought from all over the world.

Local surfer Christy Martin says Rell was one of her inspirations. "Rell Sunn touched others not just when she was alive, but even today, years after her death. I hear stories of Rell and her graceful surfing, her exploits when free diving for dinner, her sharing her love of the ocean with keiki, and of course her courage in the face of the cancer that overtook her. What I learned is that life is unpredictable, so do what you love, spread aloha, and never underestimate the effect of the ripples you send out when you live your life."

"The Aloha Spirit is real simple," Sunn often explained. "You give and you give and you give... and you give from here (the heart), until you have nothing else to give."

Rell Kapoliokaehukai Sunn.
Kapoliokaehukai means "Heart of the Sea."

I'll Remember You

One of Hawaii's greatest songwriters, Kui Lee, died of cancer in 1966.

ONE OF THE MOST beautiful love songs ever written, *I'll Remember You*, was penned by Kui Lee. Don Ho recalled the night Lee walked in with a new composition. "I sat up all night with him absorbing the essence of what he was writing about. The next day I wrote down the arrangement of the song at the club. That night I said that this was written by a friend of mine. At that time he had cancer in his throat. I sang it with the Aliis. I'll never forget that night. At that moment everybody had tears in their eyes. Then I introduced Kui. He came on stage and he sang it. Then, everybody really had tears."

I'll remember you,
Your voice as soft
As a warm summer breeze.
Your sweet laughter,

Mornings after,
Ever after, ooh,
I'll remember you.

The song was written for his wife, Nani, who had left him to live with her sister in New Jersey. Lee said it took him only 4 hours to write the song, but estimated it would earn him $500,000

Kuiokalani Lee was born in Shanghai, China, in 1932. His parents, Billy and Ethel Lee were Hawaiian musical entertainers. Following Roosevelt High School, Lee performed on the mainland as a knife dancer at the Hawaiian Room of New York's Lexington Hotel. Lee met his wife, Nani, who was a hula dancer in the show.

When his wife, Nani, left him, Kui Lee wrote "I'll Remember You" for her. Honolulu Advertiser *photos.*

Lee returned to Hawaii and for a while, was a performer and doorman at Honey's nightclub in Kaneohe — where Don Ho got his start.

Kui Lee's songs made Don Ho famous. Some of his hits included *Lahainaluna, One Paddle Two Paddle, Suck 'Em Up,* and *Ain't No Big Thing.*

Tony Bennett, the Brothers Cazimero, Andy Williams, Herb Alpert and Roger Williams are just some of the artists who have recorded his songs.

Cancer claimed the life of Kui Lee in 1966 when he was just 34.

Elvis Presley returned to Honolulu in 1973, where his *Aloha From Hawaii* concert raised $75,000 for the Kui Lee Cancer Fund. The performance was broadcast via satellite around the world to over a billion viewers.

Which Four major sports were created by Hawaii people?

Alexander Joy Cartwright moved to Hawaii in 1849 after creating baseball. He spent the rest of his life here.

FOUR MAJOR sports were created by people with ties to Hawaii. Can you name the sports?

The first is easy. Surfing. Captain Cook found Hawaiians surfing when he arrived in 1778.

The man considered the father of modern baseball, Alexander Joy Cartwright, came up with most of the rules we play by today, in 1846 in New York. He set the bases 90 feet apart, and settled on three outs per inning and nine innings per game. Three years later, in 1849, he moved to Hawaii where he spent the rest of his life.

When the Baseball Hall of Fame opened on August 26, 1939, it was declared "National Cartwright Day." Players at Ebbets Field in Brooklyn toasted him with pineapple juice. It was the first major league baseball game to be televised.

Luther Gulick Jr. is the man who encouraged the founding of the other two major indoor sports. Gulick was the son of missionaries and was born in Hawaii, but moved to Massachusetts where he was a physical education instructor at the YMCA in Springfield.

Gulick noticed that the YMCA staff was out of shape in the winter. Back in the 1890s, calesthenics were done to keep in shape during the winter, but they were boring. Gulick thought indoor games could be created using nets and balls and played in gymnasiums. He asked his students to come up with some possibilities.

Two years later, in 1891, one of his students, James

Local boy Luther Gulick, Jr., played a role in the founding of both basketball and volleyball in the 1890s.
Photo courtesy Springfield College.

Naismith came up with the idea for basketball. Five years after that, and nine miles away in Holyoke, another student, William Morgan came up with volleyball, which he originally named Mintonette, thinking it was similar to badminton.

Gulick also created the Campfire Girls and designed the YMCA logo.

So, the creation of four major sports are tied to people who had lived in Hawaii.

An Iolani Palace outside Hawaii???

A REPLICA OF IOLANI PALACE WAS ONCE built outside Hawaii. No, it wasn't built by a disgruntled prince or to fool people. Where was it? Here's a hint: It was made out of snow.

During the 1982 Sapporo Snow Festival, a huge replica of Iolani Palace was built to commemorate direct flights between Sapporo and Hawaii. The festival attracts about 2 million people a year to see hundreds of beautiful snow statues and ice sculptures, which are brilliantly lit up at night.

Amazingly, the Snow Festival was begun by local Sapporo high school students in 1950. They built six snow statues in Odori Park. Five years later, the Self-Defense Force joined in and created the very first massive snow sculpture, which now dominate the annual event.

Replicas of famous buildings are popular projects at the festival, and recent sculptures have included the Imperial Palace in Beijing, the Royal Grand Palace in Thailand, Japanese castles, the Great Wall of China, and the Parthenon in Greece. Dinosaurs, cartoon characters, and people are also fashionable.

These photos were taken by Philbert Ono, who was born and raised in Hawaii, and graduated from the University of Hawaii at Manoa. He is now based in Japan, and enjoys photographing Japanese festivals, and uploading thousands of images to his Web site at www.photoguide.jp

A replica of Iolani Palace was built out of snow in Sapporo, Japan in 1982. Photos by Philbert Ono.

Above Ala Moana in 1955

High above Honolulu in 1955, the view was drastically different than today. Magic Island was proposed that year. The Drive In still stood where Don Quijote is today. Right: Waikiki was mostly low-rise. The Ilikai was not yet built. The Hilton Lagoon had just opened. Camera Hawaii photos.

IN 1955, DILLINGHAM HIRED CAMERA HAWAII to take aerial pictures above Ala Moana Center, which was just a flat coral bed, awaiting construction at the time.

They are some of the earliest color, aerial pictures taken above Honolulu, and it was a beautiful, clear day.

Honolulu in 1955 was a very different place than it is today. It's interesting to see Ala Moana Beach Park before Magic Island was built. Henry Kaiser came up with the idea of Magic Island in 1955,

and, after 17 years of wrangling about its scope and purpose, it was completed in 1972.

Hawaii's original drive in theatre can be seen in the middle of the first picture. It was built in 1949 and was originally called simply The Drive-In. The entrance was from what is today Kaheka Street. Cars exited onto Kalakaua Avenue.

On Keeaumoku Street, Rainbow Rollerland, Scotty's Drive-In Likelike Drive Inn and a few retail shops stood, but between them and the Drive-In was mostly open fields.

When the Kam Drive In opened in 1962, Consolidated Theatres changed the theatre's name to Kapiolani Drive-In. This was a minor problem for the Kapiolani Drive-Inn restaurant (now called Wailana Coffee House), which did field a number of phone calls regarding show times.

Pacific Theatres of California bought Consolidated later that year just for the Kapiolani property. The Drive-In was quickly sold and, in 1969, Holiday Mart opened on the site. Since then, it's become Daiei and now Don Quijote.

Fifty years ago, Aloha Motors still occupied the site where the Convention Center is today. Kapiolani Coffee Shop was next door, with its famous ox-tail soup.

In 1955, the Ilikai was still nine years from construction on what was then thought to be the outskirts of Waikiki. Henry Kaiser and Fritz Burns had just purchased the old Niumalu Hotel, built in 1928, along with eight acres from the John Ena estate, and were building Kaiser's Hawaiian Village Hotel. The Hilton Lagoon had just opened.

The original plan for the Ala Wai Canal was to extend past Kapahulu to the ocean near the Natatorium, making Waikiki a true island. It looks like a good idea when seen from the air.

The Ala Moana Center foundation is ready in these 1955 photos. Magic Island only existed as an idea in the mind of visionary Henry Kaiser. The Hilton Lagoon had just opened, but the Ilikai was still 9 years from being built. Punchbowl can be seen in the distance, and the Ward Estate is visible as a green patch near the far left. Camera Hawaii photo.

Punchbowl can be seen in the top, middle of the picture above. The freeway contractor offered Stevenson Middle School a free athletic field, if he could use the fill for the "Mauka Arterial." The brown spot on Punchbowl marks its site.

The dark green area on the left is the old Ward Estate, which became the Honolulu International Center in 1967. Today it's the Neal Blaisdell Center. McKinley High School is right of that, occupying former rice fields since 1923.

When Moanalua was three times its size

MOANALUA GARDENS was developed by Samuel Mills Damon II around 1884. Back then, it was three times its present size, as this 1922 map shows.

Damon created a public park above Moanalua Road. Below it, Damon built a magnificent family estate and even had Dillingham connect a rail spur so guests could arrive in luxury for his lavish parties.

A house was built in China, disassembled, shipped to Hawaii, and reassembled near a pond close to where Servco is today. A two-story

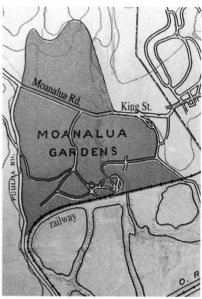

Moanalua Gardens was three times its present size, in this 1922 map The private, family area below Moanalua Road was developed into Mapunapuna in 1960.

Japanese Tea Garden, mauka of the highway, was built.

The lower part of Mapunapuna was marshland. Some parts near where Nimitz Highway is today are even below sea level. King Street began at the estate, about where Bob's Big Boy is today.

In 1960, the estate decided to develop the land makai of the highway into Mapunapuna, and many of the family structures were moved to the mauka public park.

Japan electronics giant Hitachi agreed to pay $400,000 annually to use one of the garden's famous monkeypod trees as its logo. It attracts hundreds of tourists a week.

Why was it named the Tahitian Lanai?

SPENCECLIFF RESTAURANTS opened the Tahitian Lanai in 1956. While on a vacation to Tahiti, Spence Weaver fell in love with a dancer at his hotel. To show his love for her, Spence opened a restaurant with a Tahitian theme, and decorated it with materials he brought back from Tahiti.

What girl cannot help but fall for a guy who opens a restaurant in her honor? Turere could not, and she was soon his wife.

The Tahitian Lanai was at the Waikikian Hotel, with some tables around the pool, and others in private grass huts. They were famous for their banana muffins and Eggs Benedict. Restaurateur Fred Livingston was the owner at one time and still serves those famous dishes on weekends at his new place, the Tower Grill at Aloha Tower Marketplace.

The Tahitian Lanai was once one of Honolulu's top restaurants. Bishop Museum photos.

Where is the Space Shuttle emergency landing site in Hawaii?

ALTHOUGH IT HAS NEVER HAD TO BE USED, a Hawaii landing site was created should the Space Shuttle need to make an emergency landing in the North Pacific. We know it as the Reef Runway.

Normally, the Space Shuttle lands at Cape Canaveral, Florida, or Andrews Air Force Base in California.

Many landing strips around the world have been designated emergency landing sites for the Space Shuttle, including the Reef Runway.

The Honolulu International Airport runway 8R was built in 1977 at a cost of $80 million. It was the first runway to be built entirely off-shore.

The Reef Runway is an emergency landing site for the Space Shuttle.

What was the Ala Wai Golf Course's original name?

THE ALA WAI GOLF COURSE began in 1923 as part of the Territorial Fairgrounds. While most golf courses are planned and then built, the Ala Wai began as a single hole in 1923 and evolved into an 18 hole course over the next 14 years.

Sam Yap and Babe Carter are credited with planting a simple salmon can in the ground near the present site of hole number six.

In 1924, prisoners helped build three more holes and the Territorial Fairgrounds Golf Course opened to the public. A "round" cost 25¢.

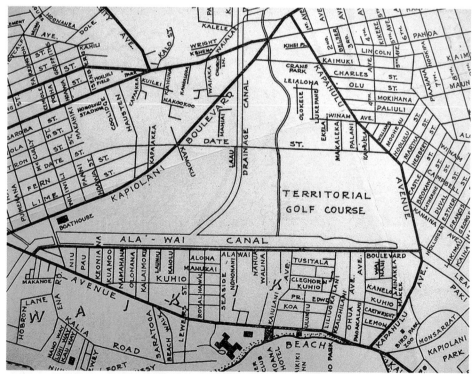

The Ala Wai Golf Course began in 1923 with a single hole as the Territorial Fairgrounds Golf Course.

The Ala Wai Golf Course is one of the busiest in the world. Photo courtesy Belt-Collins.

By 1931, the course expanded to nine, then to 18 holes in 1937. It was Hawaii's first municipal course.

The Territorial Fairgrounds baseball stadium, grandstands, and horse racing track were crowded out by the growing golf course.

Various politicians have suggested the land be used for other purposes, such as Aloha Stadium, the Convention Center or hotels. Japanese investors once offered $2 billion for the land.

Over 180,000 rounds of play are tallied each year, making the Ala Wai one of the busiest golf courses in the world.

The Ho House

THERE SHOULD BE A HAWAIIAN PRESIDENT, Don Ho believed. He volunteered for the job. "President Ho," he suggested. "And I'd move the White House to Hawaii, and call it the Ho House."

Newscaster Linda Coble said that when she moved to Hawaii in 1969, she often went to the Don Ho Show at Duke's. "I'd sit in the Harem Section," she recalls. "The first row was for hot coeds — locals, and those fresh off the plane like me."

Coble estimates she saw hundreds of his shows. "I was there almost every night for my first few months here." Three to four hundred attended his shows.

Unlike most performers, more than half of Don's shows were banter with the audience. It was probably why he was so successful. He engaged the audience and invited them to participate.

"He was magical with everybody," Coble says, "The Harem Section, the honeymooners, people celebrating their anniversaries. He'd have them get up and either sing a song, tell a joke, or buy the house a round."

"They were given a spot light," Coble continues. "The grandmas would sing *New York New York, Tiny Bubbles,* or some song. Everybody had

Don's mother, Honey, wife Melva, and Don in 1980. Honolulu Advertiser *photos.*

a moment. Don could look across the organ and make a connection with people in the audience. Everyone felt special at his shows."

Linda and Don were so close and friendly through the years, that after boyfriend Kirk Matthews moved to Hawaii in 1983, and wanted to marry Linda, he had to sit on Don's lap and ask permission.

"I came back from two years in Portland with a haole boy," Coble says. "I was told I shouldn't get married to him until Don checked him out."

Don looked him over and must have liked him, but he had a warning: "If you evah hurt dis girl, I'm gonna kill you."

Coble remembers Don joking about his first bus ride on the mainland when he joined the Air Force. Blacks had to sit in the

back of the bus in the South back then, but, while he looked different, they didn't know what to make of him.

"They'd look at me, and look at me and nevah knew what to do with me. I'd end up sitting in da *middle* of the bus," Don would joke.

Was there a fort on Fort Street?

Fort Street was named for a fort built on the waterfront in 1815 by Russian traders.

RUSSIAN FUR TRADERS began coming to the islands around 1804 for fruit, vegetables and meat.

Without the knowledge or permission of Czar Alexander I, Captain Yury Lisyansky, commander of the ship *Neva* considered taking over Hawaii.

The Russians built a fort at Honolulu Harbor and another, whose remains can be seen today near Waimea, Kauai.

The fort was built in 1815. On the advice of John Young, Kamehameha I expelled the Russians from the fort.

With walls 16 feet in height, it was once Hawaii's largest structure. Hawaiian Historical Society photos.

Oahu Governor John Adams Kuakini rebuilt the fort and extended its walls to a height of 16 feet. It was the largest structure in the islands at the time.

By 1857, the fort was in disrepair and was torn down. Most of the rubble was dropped into Honolulu Harbor to extend it. Some of it is still visible in the waters off Nimitz Highway across from the Amfac building.

Fort Street began at the fort, about where Nimitz Highway is today and extended all the way to Pacific Heights Drive. It was Hawaii's first paved street, around 1898.

Which Asian War led to the U.S. Annexation of Hawaii?

WHEN THE HAWAIIAN MONARCHY was overthrown in 1893, officials asked the U.S. to annex Hawaii as a territory. Grover Cleveland was President and a friend of Queen Liliuokalani. He opposed annexation. William McKinley became President and supported annexation in 1898.

The factor that changed in those five years was the Spanish American War. It was fought mainly in the Philippines, and in Cuba, led by General William Shafter. All of a sudden, Hawaii's location became strategically important to the United States.

If not for the Spanish-American War, Hawaii would probably not have been annexed when it was. In fact, annexation may have never taken place.

Hawaii would probably not have been annexed by the U.S. in 1898 if not for the Spanish-American War. All of a sudden, Hawaii became strategically important. The Battle of Manilla, 1898. *Library of Congress*

Who was the first president to visit Papakolea?

Franklin Roosevelt was the first U.S. President to visit Hawaii.
Honolulu Advertiser *photos.*

FRANKLIN D. Roosevelt was the first president to visit Hawaii, in 1934. His began his trip in Hilo, where he planted the first tree on what has become Banyan Drive.

He drove to Kilauea Crater in his open touring car and threw some ohelo berries to Madame Pele.

On Oahu, he held a parade in Pearl City, dedicated Ala Moana Beach Park, paid a visit to Shriner's Hospital, and met with the commanders of Schofield Barracks and Pearl Harbor. Every president since FDR has visited Hawaii, but most likely, none have gone to Papakolea.

Papakolea was initially populated with native Hawaiian squatters who were pushed out of downtown's overcrowded slums. By executive order, Roosevelt made Papakolea a part of Hawaiian Homelands. Papakolea is named for the Kolea — a plover bird — that used to migrate through the area.

Why would the President be concerned with the standard of living of Hawaiians? Some believe Roosevelt was concerned with the plight of the poor everywhere. He would later chastise

Pres. Roosevelt planted this Kukui tree, just Ewa of the Palace, in 1934.

Winston Churchill for England's failure to improve the lives of native peoples in its empire.

Coincidentally, nearby Roosevelt High School is not named for FDR but for his distant cousin, Theodore Roosevelt. The school opened just 4 years earlier, in 1930 across the street from the present campus, on what is now Stevenson Intermediate.

Before returning to Washington D.C., FDR dined with Governor Poindexter, and planted a kukui tree at Iolani Palace. The plaque says: "President Franklin D. Roosevelt planted this kukui tree July 28, 1934." The tree can be found just ewa of the palace.

The Kukui tree Roosevelt planted 60 years ago is now over 30 feet tall and is considered lucky. Some credit Roosevelt's winning the elections of 1936, 1940 and 1944 to the Lucky Kukui Tree.

The President delivered a seven-minute speech from the Iolani Palace balcony to the crowd below. Listeners on the radio heard him say:

President Roosevelt brought his own convertible touring car, and made speeches from it

"I leave you today with reluctance, for the friendly spirit and the generous reception given me everywhere by the people of the Islands of the Territory makes me greatly wish that my visit could be prolonged.

"And so, my friends, I leave you my gratitude for all the kindnesses you have shown me. I carry with me the hope that I shall have the opportunity to return.

"My friends, I shall ever remember these days — days that are all too short — your flowers, your scenery, your hospitality, but, above all, the knowledge that America can well be proud of the Territory of Hawaii. And so I say to you: Aloha from the bottom of my heart."

Which church has Jesus surfing in its stained glass window?

MANY CHURCHES have intricate stained glass windows with biblical scenes portrayed in brilliantly colored mosaics of light. But only one might show Jesus on a surfboard.

The church is St. Andrews Cathedral on Beretania Street. The entrance to the church facing the street and the fountain is a fifty-foot tall wall of glass.

When it was installed in the late 1950s, it was one of the largest ever constructed in the United States. John Wallis of Pasadena, California was the designer.

Jesus is surfing to heaven on St. Andrew's Cathedral's stained glass window.

When asked why he put Jesus on a surfboard, he just smiled.

The window portrays over thirty biblical scenes, including the birth of Jesus, the Last Supper, pyramids representing the flight into Egypt, Mary and Joseph, and John the Baptist.

King Kamehameha IV and his Queen, Emma are portrayed on the right panel. They are the founders of the cathedral. Both visited Queen Victoria of England and requested support in bringing the Anglican Church of England to Hawaii.

St. Andrew was Jesus' first disciple. Kamehameha IV died on his Feast Day at the young age of 29 in the church's first year, as the cathedral was being built. Originally it was going to be dedicated to St. Peter, but Prince Lot, Kamehameha V chose to honor his brother and St. Andrew. Coincidentally, Peter and Andrew were also brothers.

St. Andrew's white cross against a blue background is also part of Hawaii's flag, along with St. George's and St. Patrick's crosses.

The glass is all-hand blown, from France, Germany, England and the U.S. The wall was a gift from Louise Gaylord Dillingham in honor of her mother.

The new church's first Bishop, Thomas Staley is depicted on the wall. His first service in Hawaii was October 12, 1862. Less than a month later, two services were

King Kamehameha IV and Queen Emma, who brought the church to Hawaii, can be found on the stained glass window's lower right panel. The King died on the Feast Day of Saint Andrew and the church's name was made to honor that.

conducted, one in Hawaiian and one in English, a tradition that continues to this day.

The wall has one further unique aspect — a stained glass termite. Some of the credit for building the wall is given to the termites who ate much of the older wooden structures, necessitating a restoration. One was "honored" at the bottom right of the wall.

Right: The Last Supper is one of over 30 Biblical events shown in the stained glass window, shown as a whole, below.

Which Punahou boy discovered
Machu Picchu?

A PUNAHOU graduate discovered the Lost City of the Incas in 1911 and was a model for the fictional character Indiana Jones. Who was this Hawaii boy?

Local boy Hiram Bingham III discovered the Lost City of the Incas in 1911. Wikipedia Commons photos.

He was Hiram Bingham III. His grandfather founded both Kawaiahao Church and Punahou School. The grandson was born here in 1875 and followed in his father's and grandfather's footsteps and became an ordained minister. However, the tradewinds blew a private schooner into Honolulu, and the young Bingham fell in love, says a distant cousin, Charles Montague Black, who owns Furniture Plus Design at the Gentry Pacific Center.

The schooner belonged to the Mitchell's, heirs to the Tiffany fortune. They didn't want their daughter marrying an itinerant preacher and kept them apart. Undaunted, Bingham left the priesthood, and got a masters in history from U.C. Berkeley. He became curator of both Harvard and Yale's South American libraries.

He married Alfreda Mitchell, granddaughter of Charles Tiffany, in 1899, and had seven sons with her.

While in Peru to study South American people and plants, and to collect books, Bingham was told of ruins high above them in the Andes.

With just one guide, Bingham made the trek up to the 13,000-foot peak and discovered what is today considered one of the wonders of the modern world, Machu Picchu (which means "old peak").

Charles Black, who took 16 relatives there in 2001 for the 90th anniversary of its discovery says Bingham found it overgrown with vines. However, what he could see was amazing - over 140 dwellings, temples, and roads. It even had waterways that entered each dwelling.

"There were many llamas there, and most of them are taller than six feet and not very friendly," Black recounts. "They run freely over the entire site and clip the grass. They can reach spots inaccessible to lawn mowers. I called them 'llama-mowers.'"

Machu Picchu was constructed at the height of the Incan empire around 1450 AD. Even though it is less than 50 miles from the Incan capital, Cusco, the Spanish conquistadors never discovered it in their search for gold.

Hiram Bingham III was the model for the fictional character Indiana Jones.

Bingham coined the name "The Lost City of the Incas," which was the title of his first book. Bingham was one of the people that inspired George Lucas to create the fictional character, Indiana Jones. Harrison Ford wore another cousin's hat and jacket in the movie.

Hiram Bingham IV also distinguished himself. During World War II, as a U.S. diplomat in France, he helped over 2,500 Jews escape Nazi persecution.

How the Polynesian Cultural Center grew out of a Waikiki performing group

T HE POLYNESIAN CULTURAL CENTER has the distinction of beginning as a group of performers called the Polynesian Panorama.

The Polynesian Panorama was a group of South Pacific students who began performing traditional songs and dances in Waikiki in 1959 at the International Market Place.

The group moved to Kaiser's Hawaiian Village Hotel, and by 1961 were selling out the Waikiki Shell. Tourists could not get enough of them.

The Polynesian Cultural Center developed out of The Polynesian Panorama, a group that performed in Waikiki.

At the time, the Church College of Hawaii in Laie was just 5 years old. Many of the students needed money and, while local students could find jobs, international students had fewer options.

The Church College leaders thought they could create a home for the Polynesian Panorama in Laie. It could merge with a community hukilau program and occupy a 15 acre site next to the college. The "Polynesian Village," as it was first called took the form of little villages that represented different South Pacific islands. Much of it was built by volunteers, many of whom came at their own expense, such as over 100 Maori from New Zealand.

Queen Salote of Tonga sent several master builders to help construct a scale model of her summer palace.

The new Polynesian Cultural Center in 1964 was a lot smaller than it is today. Honolulu Advertiser *photo.*

Millions of Malasadas

Some of our restaurants and bakeries sell staggering amounts of one particular, signature item. Few ever stop to count how many they've made since they began. HPU student Brandi Boatner did some legwork and calculations. Here are some estimates of the total number some of our companies have sold.

Zippy's Chili

175 million servings since 1963.

Leonard's Malasadas

150 million since 1952

Liliha Bakery Coco puffs

20 million since 1990.

Royal Kitchen Baked Manapua

13 million since 1975

Matsumoto's shave ice

12 million since 1951

Big Kahuna's Garlic Cheese Balls

7 million since 1994

Boulevard Saimin

6 million bowls since 1951

Helena's Hawaiian Food Pipikaula Short Ribs

1 million since 1987

Joe Moore – The slowest speaking newscaster in Hawaii .

Early days at Aiea High School

Everyone who watches KHON knows Joe Moore went to Aiea High School. "I don't tell a lot of people – unless it comes up," Joe says. "I just don't volunteer it because I love my Aiea connection. I went there three years – freshman, sophomore and junior."

"The first year they opened the school, I went in as a freshman. I would have been in the first graduating class to go all four years, but my dad got transferred out of Hickam, so I wasn't here for my senior year."

"I wanted to stay, the coach and principal came to the house, to try and convince my dad to let me stay. I was captain of the football team and student body president."

"My dad took me for a ride, and said 'Ok, you're old enough,

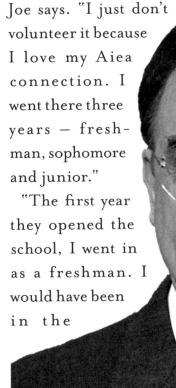

Joe Moore has been KHON anchor since 1980.

I'm going to let you make this decision.' And I'm sitting there going 'Yes!'"

"Then he said, 'I just want you to remember one thing — this is the last year your mother and your brother and you and I will be together as a family, and you know what this will do to your mother,' and by this time I'm bawling like a baby. 'Ok, I'll go with you guys.'"

"I hardly remember that last year in Ohio. It's my three years at Aiea I remember fondly."

Breaking into broadcasting

At the University of Maryland, Joseph Brice Moore, Jr. found himself at the campus radio station. When the play-by-play guy needed help during a football game he turned to Joe, who discovered he enjoyed that line of work. "By the end of the first half, I was talking on the radio as much as the play-by-play guy. And I thought, this is a snap. This is great. I've got a new career here."

Joe Moore reveals the secret to his success and longevity at KHON.

After his sophomore year, Joe joined the army and served two tours in Vietnam, where he worked as a broadcast journalist covering news of the 25th Infantry Division.

When he got out in 1969, he wrote a letter to KGMB and was hired as a sportscaster for $2.75 an hour.

Joe worked with Bob Sevey from 1969-1978 at KGMB. "Bob was like a second father to me," Joe says. "My dad was off on the mainland. As a young guy in the business, I looked up to him and turned to him for advice. He was definitely my #1 mentor."

Clowning around

Joe was known to clown around on the set in his early days. Linda Coble recalls his Evel Knievel impersonation, on camera, riding a tricycle across from the sports desk to the news desk (see page 68).

"When I was first a sportscaster, I was just out of the service and in my 20s. I could be more of a clown. When Mohammed Ali fought Joe Frazier I said I had the perfect defense for Frazier and came out wearing a trash can."

"I swung on a rope through the set dressed as Tarzan when someone had rescued somebody. But when I moved over to news I stopped it. You don't want your news guy being a clown. My *Finally tonight, did you know* thing, is now the way I end the news on a lighter note."

Moving from sports to news anchor

In 1978, Joe moved from #1 ranked KGMB to the #3 station, KHON where he continued covering sports. Paul Udell was anchor there, but in 1980, abruptly decided to leave.

"Bill Snyder, our general manager came to me and said, what do you think of being news anchor instead of sports? It struck me out of the blue," Moore recounts. "I had not thought about it at all."

"I had drawn up a proposal to do a combination Johnny Carson, Phil Donahue talk show, kind of what Andy Bumatai is doing now. I was feeling a little burned out in sports."

"I took the weekend and came back and told him I thought being news anchor would be a good career move and wanted to do it. It wasn't a huge leap for me because I was always interested in civics and history. I'd get up in the morning and read the paper, and news periodicals such as *Newsweek* and *Time*."

"After the first week as news anchor, Snyder came to me and said, 'Joe, I'm not complaining, but you're sort of taking on this Cronkite thing that doesn't quite seem to be you."

"So I watched the air checks. And I thought, son of a gun. I thought I was just being a little more serious. It wasn't Walter Cronkite. To me I thought my style was like a cross between John Wayne and David Brinkley. It's not intentional." Joe then takes on their personas:

"It's not ... EXACTLY ... the way ... David BRINKLEY ... would do a STORY ... because ... that would be ... PHONY ... I won't DO it ... and nobody would ... WATCH."

"But there's a little bit of the Duke in there: because he ... would pause in places where ... you wouldn't ... think that he would ... and then HIT IT hard. I do like to hit some words harder than others."

The secret of his success

"I've never told anyone this, but now that I'm at the tail end of my career, I can give away my secret; because people ask: What's the secret to your success and longevity?"

"It's very, very simple, and I never wanted to share it before because I didn't want other news anchors to know. It's so simple they're all going to think (hits his head) of course!"

"Well now, I'm 60 years old. I'm at the tail end of my career, more power to them. It would be better for the audience if they all knew and copied this."

"Speak slowly. That's the secret. Every news director I ever worked for has said, 'come on, speed it up, we can get another 3-4 stories in there if you would just pick up the pace.'"

"And I say, you know what, the guys at the other stations are doing that. Do you want to have their ratings? I'm convinced, especially our older audience, watches when I'm anchoring because I speak slowly. I enunciate, and once you get older and a little hard of hearing, you only have one chance to hear it. It's not like a newspaper, where you can read it again."

"So I've always deliberately spoken very slowly. I may be the slowest speaking newscaster in the country. It's by design. And I'm convinced that's a major part of my success and longevity with this station."

How Les Keiter became "The General"

How "The General," Les Keiter, got his nickname. Honolulu Advertiser *photo.*

"Les and I had done a *Hawaii Five-0* episode and I played an army captain and he played an army general. We worked at rival stations. I was at Ch. 9 and he was at Ch. 2. I saw him a week later at the old Honolulu Stadium and yelled out across the field, 'hey General!'"

"He later told me that regulars at the stadium, when they'd see him walk by, started calling him

Chuck Leahey was famous for saying "third down and a manapua to go!" Honolulu Advertiser *photo.*

General and saluting him. He had that military bearing and a command presence voice, and the nickname just stuck."

"At first, he didn't like people calling him that because he had been in the navy. He would have been happier if people called him 'Admiral.' But he came to really like it after awhile."

When Joe became anchor at KHON in 1980, Les was his sportscaster. "He and I were out there as a team for years. I loved working with him. There was that something. I think I have that again with Kanoa Leahey. It feels right. It was that way with Les."

"I was the younger guy with Sevey and Keiter. It's interesting for me, now that I'm the old guy with these younger guys. It's a nice little circular deal."

Joe recalls how Kanoa's grandfather, Chuck Leahey had one of the greatest all time football sayings. "No one who heard it will ever forget — 'third down and a manapua to go for the first!' he'd say."

Bryce

Joe has a daughter by his first marriage, JoAnn, in Chicago and two grandchildren. "My wife Teresa and I were blessed with a son unexpectedly. We had tried for seven years, and couldn't get pregnant. We were considering *in vitro* and planned to discuss it after a vacation.

"While we were at the Savoy Hotel in London, she came out of the bathroom with a pregnancy test kit and said, 'does this look blue to you?' and I said, 'oh my God, yes.'"

"And she says, 'I don't know, it doesn't look blue to me.'"

"And I said, 'honey, that's blue.'"

"My wife and I had said from Day One that we wanted a boy, and if we got a boy, we're stopping. When we saw the ultrasound, and that it was a boy, we were so happy we were both bawling like babies."

Joseph Brice Moore Sr., Joe's father has, as his middle name, the doctor's name that delivered him – Dr. Brice. Joseph Brice Moore Jr. named his son Bryce. "We changed the spelling for him. When I told my dad that, he said, 'you mean like the damned canyon?'"

"Yeah, dad, like the damned canyon."

Bryce was nine in 2007. What do they like to do together? "We do a lot of swimming in the pool. I try to keep up with him at basketball and soccer. I love going to the movies with him. Just helping him learn to read and write and all that stuff. He helped me rehearse my lines in *Prophecy and Honor*."

His future in broadcasting

Where most TV anchors have one and two-year contracts, Joe has an unprecedented 14-year contract that expires in 2009. Will he retire when it's over?

"My original intention was to go until 62, so that's another couple of years. But with Bryce, now I'm thinking I may go until I am 65."

"But I'm leaving that option open. We'll see how things are going in two years; who owns the station and what kind of owner they are. Sixty-five is sounding more and more like a good game plan to me. But who knows in this business. It's changed so much."

—Researched by Cathy Handen

Who revived interest in the ukulele in the 1950s?

Arthur Godfrey is largely credited with reviving America's interest in the ukulele in the 1950s. Honolulu Advertiser *photos.*

IN 1879, PORTU-GUESE immigrants from the Madeira Islands brought a musical instrument, called the braguinha, with them to Hawaii. This quickly evolved into the ukulele, whose name means "jumping flea," possibly for how quickly a player's fingers moved.

The ukulele was introduced to the world at the Panama-Pacific Exposition, held in San Francisco in 1915. The Hawaiian exhibit was well received and America embraced the ukulele and Hawaiian music. By 1916, Hawaiian records were the top-selling genre in the U.S.

Interest in the ukulele faded during the 1930s, but one man is largely credited with reviving interest in it. His name was Arthur Godfrey. Godfrey had come to Hawaii during World War II as a correspondent and spent a lot of time at the Willows restaurant. Stranded here temporarily, Godfrey said that "those great people took me in, didn't know who I was and didn't care. I went back full of love for this place and couldn't get it out of my system."

After World War II, his *Arthur Godfrey's Talent Scouts* TV show became a huge hit. Between acts, Godfrey, wearing an aloha shirt would play a song on the ukulele. Tony Bennett, Patsy Cline, Pat Boone, and many others were

Arthur Godfrey fell in love with Hawaii during World War II. He and Duke became best friends. Honolulu Advertiser *photo, taken by Nadine Kahanamoku.*

"discovered" on the show. Elvis Presley tried out and was rejected!

Indirectly, the aloha spirit that Willow's owner Kathleen Perry showed Godfrey led to a renaissance for the ukulele in the U.S.

Duke Kahanamoku and Godfrey became close friends. They made a promise to each other, that whoever lived the longest would attend the other's funeral. In 1968, Arthur Godfrey delivered the eulogy at Duke's funeral.

Neil Young has said he became interested in music at age seven, when his father gave him an Arthur Godfrey ukulele.

Godfrey felt the ukelele was more than a musical instrument. "If a kid has a uke in his hands, he is not going to get into much trouble."

Who is famous for sailing his airplane to Hawaii?

The seaplane Commander John Rodgers flew and then sailed to Hawaii in 1925, shown flying off Oahu after it had been repaired. Smithsonian Institution photo.

T HIS EARLY AVIATOR WAS THE FIRST TO attempt a non-stop flight from California to Hawaii. His five-man crew left San Francisco in a seaplane on August 31, 1925. Three planes were scheduled to fly together. One needed repairs and was scratched. Another turned back after just 200 miles, leaving just one, under the command of Captain John Rodgers.

The PN-9 plane was so heavy, one of the pilots later said, "we had to fly fifty miles before we could climb to 300 feet." Had the Golden Gate Bridge been built, the plane would have had to fly under it. The famous bridge opened in 1937.

In calculating fuel requirements, the Navy anticipated

tradewinds that failed to materialize. The seaplane could have refueled, if it could have found
waiting supply ships, but poor communications
prevented that from happening

When the seaplane ran out of fuel, it landed in
rough waters and waited for nearby ships to find
them. However, the crew discovered the radio
transmitter needed the propellers spinning to
generate electricity. The seaplane could receive
messages, but not send.

John Rodgers

The searchers were looking for the plane to their south. At one
point, they came within 5 miles of a merchant ship and lit a fire
in a bucket of oily rags to create black smoke. With the morning
sun behind them, the seaplane went unseen.

Commander John Rodgers and his crew improvised two sails
from the planes' fabric-covered wings and hung them between
the engines. A wooden rudder was used to steer toward Hawaii. It
worked. The sails billowed and caught the wind. Rodgers calculated
they were 350 miles east of the islands.

After four days, the crew ran out of food and water. On the
seventh day, they took down the sails in a squall and used them to
catch three quarts of water. The water, and sighting Oahu improved
their morale, although Rodgers calculated they were 50 miles away
and drifting on a course that would take them west of Oahu.

Rogers decided to attempt a landing on Kauai instead, fearing
they might pass through the channel between it an Oahu, if they

tried to make landfall on Oahu.

After sailing the plane for nine days, the seaplane and crew were found 15 miles off Nawiliwili Bay, Kauai by a submarine.

The fliers were welcomed on Kauai by nearly the entire population of Lihue, then met with Governor Farrington on Oahu. Cmdr. Rodgers handed him a letter — the first ever to arrive in Hawaii by air.

During the time the plane was drifting at sea, another airship disaster occurred — a dirigible, the *Shenandoah* went down in a thunderstorm in the Midwest. The captain had been ordered to fly despite the storm. Fourteen crew members were lost.

These two incidents outraged Col. Billy Mitchell, who fought the Army and Navy to create a separate Air Force. His concern was that the Army and Navy under-funded the air corps and neglected safety concerns.

When reporters asked for his comments he told them "these accidents are the direct result of the incompetency, criminal negligence and almost treasonable administration of the national defense by the Navy and War Departments." Mitchell was court-martialed for his insubordination.

KHON anchorman, Joe Moore, who wrote the play, *Prophecy & Honor* about the court martial, believed Mitchell felt a trial would allow him to publicize his concerns, and expected punishment to be light, but was instead forced to resign his commission.

Cmdr. Rodgers was killed in a plane crash a year later on August 27, 1926. Honolulu opened its first full airport in March of 1927 and named it for the man who flew then sailed his airplane to Hawaii. Twenty years later, in 1947, it was renamed Honolulu International Airport. The John Rodgers Terminal building was dedicated in 1962.

Who was the first Hawaiian to pitch for the Baltimore Orioles?

"RUSTY," AS HE WAS KNOWN, was one of the finest all-around island born athletes in the early part of the 1920s. In his freshman year at the University of Hawaii, he quarterbacked "Proc" Klum's Fighting Deans, as they were then called.

Neal Blaisdell was the driving force behind building Aloha Stadium. Honolulu Advertiser *photo.*

He played basketball and was a good enough southpaw pitcher to earn a job with the 1926 Baltimore Orioles. Oh, and he was elected Mayor of Honolulu 5 times. Who was he?

He was Neal Shaw Blaisdell. The last of seven children, Blaisdell was born in 1902, the son of an Irish fireman. His mother was part Hawaiian, the granddaughter of John Adams Cummins, the minister of foreign affairs under King Kalakaua.

Is there a relation between Neal Blaisdell and the Blaisdell Hotel? Yes. His grandmother, Mrs. William Wallace Blaisdell operated the hotel from 1910 until 1913. Neal earned 25 cents a week scrubbing hallways, running errands and doing chores at the hotel when he was 10 years old.

Blaisdell attended Kamehameha and Saint Louis, and lettered in football, baseball and basketball. He graduated in 1921 and went on to the University of Hawaii and Bucknell College, before spending a season pitching for the Baltimore Orioles.

He came home to Hawaii and became a football and basketball coach at McKinley from 1927-31, then at Roosevelt, Punahou and

Saint Louis from 1943-49. At the same time, Blaisdell worked for Bishop Trust and Hawaiian Pineapple, where he was both personnel and recreation director.

He was elected to the Territorial legislature in 1944 and 1946 as an independent Republican, but a bout of tuberculosis landed him in Leahi Hospital for 7 months.

"In the hospital, I had a lot of time to think," Blaisdell recalled. "I felt I could contribute something to the City. It was nothing great or dramatic, just a feeling that there was room for a person of my training in the business world and my familiarity with local needs."

He lost his first race for mayor in 1952, but won two-year terms in 1954, '56, and '58 and four year terms in 1960 and '64. During that time, he guided the City and County of Honolulu from a small town of 350,000 to a major metropolis of more than 650,000.

Realtor Rick Ornellas recalls caddying for Blaisdell several times at the Oahu Country Club in 1962. "Blaisdell was a gentleman," Ornellas says. "He had a sweet disposition and wasn't arrogant at all. I loved that guy."

"On one occasion, he gave me a 50 cent tip and said, 'here kid. Buy yourself a cigar.' He was joking with me. I was just 14 at the time." Ornellas would get $2.50 (about $16 in today's dollars) to carry two golf bags for 18 holes, so 50 cents was good money.

In 1965, Blaisdell began the process that eventually resulted in the construction of Aloha Stadium. He was also the driving force that led to the building of the Honolulu International Center, now named Neal S. Blaisdell Center. Blaisdell retired in 1968 and passed away in 1975.

"Honolulu will forever be in his debt," said Governor William Quinn "for the leadership he gave her as statehood and the jet age gave rise to incredible growth and change."

Who was Duke Kahanamoku named for?

PRINCE ALFRED, the second son of Queen Victoria came to Hawaii in 1869 on a tour of the Pacific. King Kamehameha V was embarrassed because there was no decent place for him to stay, except private homes and rooms above saloons.

The prince stayed with Queen Emma, who had twice visited England, at her Summer Palace in Nuuanu.

Duke and Nadine Kahanamoku at a press conference following surgery he had in 1962. Honolulu Advertiser *photo*

The King encouraged the building of a hotel downtown across from Iolani Palace, that became the Royal Hawaiian Hotel.

That same year, a baby was born downtown in Bernice Pauahi Bishop's home. She suggested he be named in honor of the visit of Prince Alfred, the Duke of Edinburgh.

Duke Kahanamoku was named after Prince Alfred, the Duke of Edinburgh. Hawaii State Archives photo

Twenty-one years later, in 1890, Duke Halapu Kahanamoku and his wife had a son, also born in the Bishop's home downtown. He was named Duke Paoa Kahanamoku.

Few today seem to know that Duke Kahanamoku was named for a real duke.

The Biggest Tinker Toy set in town

A FASCINATING FACT ABOUT IOLANI PALACE was uncovered during renovations in 1983. When ironworkers took apart the ornamental fence to clean and paint it, they discovered there wasn't a weld in them.

The half a mile of fencing was machined so well that it has stood solidly for over 100 years without a weld. Arc-welding was invented 20 years after the fence went up. The workers back then crafted square posts and holes, and each section fit so snugly that none came loose, even after a century in the elements.

Ironworker Alex Klahm called it the biggest Tinker Toy set in town. "The whole thing fit together like a child's toy."

The Iolani Palace gates were called the Biggest Tinker Toy Set in Hawaii. Honolulu Advertiser *Photo.*

The last Spencecliff restaurant

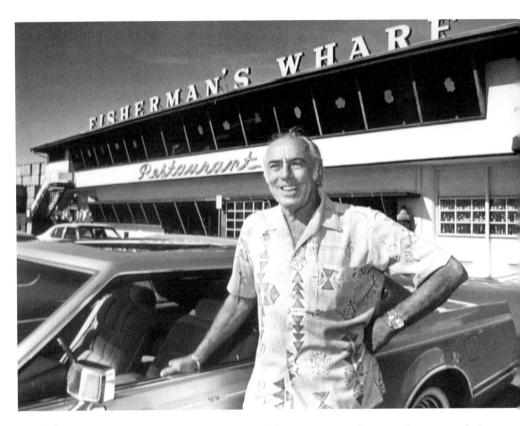

S PENCECLIFF WAS OAHU'S most popular and successful restaurant chain from the 1940s through the 1970s. They owned over 50 restaurants, including Coco's, Tahitian Lanai, Ranch House, Kelly's Coffee Shop, Queen's Surf, and Trader Vics

Only one restaurant remains. Fisherman's Wharf. Co-founder Spence Weaver posed outside it in the 1950s. In 1986, Nittaku Corporation bought Spencecliff for $6 million, but losses forced them to close restaurants until only Fisherman's Wharf remains today.

—*Researched by Ilima Guerrero*

What were the alternative names and possible locations for Aloha Stadium?

I T TOOK almost 20 years for the idea of a large stadium to replace Honolulu Stadium to come to fruition.

Mayor Neal S. Blaisdell first proposed it in 1958. Fire department leaders said the old "Termite Palace" was a firetrap. Sporting and other events had been held at the old

Over 600 families once lived in Halawa, where Aloha Stadium would be built. Honolulu Advertiser *photos.*

Honolulu Stadium on King Street since it opened in 1936, but it was felt that a growing city needed a bigger stadium.

Between 1958 and 1975, many locations and names were considered.

The Ala Wai Golf Course site was considered, as was the U.H.

The Halawa Stadium under construction in 1974

Quarry, Diamond Head Crater, Kapiolani Park, McKinley High School, Sand Island and Keehi Lagoon Park were nominated, before a Citizen's Stadium Committee selected Halawa. Six hundred families that lived in the area had to be relocated.

Possible names for the new stadium included Poi Bowl, Pineapple Bowl, and John A. Burns Stadium..

Originally, it was called the Halawa Stadium. The *Honolulu Advertiser* held a "Name the Stadium" contest in 1974. Over 10,000 names were submitted, including, Poi Bowl, Pineapple Bowl, Aloharena, and John A. Burns Stadium.

Aloha Stadium won the most votes — 441. In 1975, it was official. The name Halawa Stadium was dropped and it became Aloha Stadium. The old Honolulu Stadium closed down in 1974 and was torn down in 1976. The area was turned into a park.

The Hawaii Islanders AAA baseball team took up residence at Aloha Stadium for 13 years, until moving to Colorado Springs in 1987. Barry Bonds played briefly on the team in 1986 before being called up by the Pirates.

Aloha Stadium has hosted the National Football League's Pro Bowl since 1980.

Aloha Stadium has also hosted huge concerts, including The Eagles, The Police, The Rolling Stones, Celine Dion, Mariah Carey and Michael Jackson.

From the same angle as the first picture, Aloha Stadium today.

143

The "Bambino" plays ball in Hilo

George Herman "Babe" Ruth arriving in Hilo.

THE MOST POPULAR athlete of his time, Babe Ruth came to play an exhibition baseball game at Ho'olulu Park in Hilo on Oct. 29, 1933.

Ruth, his wife Claire, and daughter Julia, came to Hawaii for two weeks where he played exhibition games in Honolulu and Hilo.

The greatest day in Hilo baseball history was when Babe Ruth came to play.

In Hilo, the Waiakea Pirates played an "all-star" team composed of Ruth and some of the best players on the Big Island.

When Ruth arrived at the stadium, he found over 200 kids waiting outside, unable to afford the 25 cent admission.

Ruth threw open the gates and invited the kids into the outfield, while he took batting practice. He offered to autograph any ball they caught.

Soon the Pirates took the field and the game was

Ruth's All-Stars.

under way. The crowd came to see Babe Ruth hit a home run, and he didn't disappoint them. He hit two, but his All-Stars lost to the Waiakea Pirates 7-6. It didn't matter. It

"All set to smack for a homer."

was one of the greatest games ever played in Hilo, just because Babe Ruth came to play.

While he was in Hilo, Babe Ruth planted a banyan tree on Hilo's Walk of Fame. Today, it is directly in front of the Hilo Hawaiian Hotel.

More than 50 celebrities and political leaders have planted banyan trees there, including President Franklin D. Roosevelt, Amelia Earhart, filmmaker Cecil B. deMille, and trumpeter Louis Armstrong.

Ruth's second home run went 427 feet.

Ruth's real name was George Herman Ruth. His Baltimore Orioles teammates gave him the nickname "Babe." He was also called the Bambino and Sultan of Swat.

The pictures on this page were put

The Waiakea Pirates beat Ruth's All-Stars 7-6.

into a scrapbook by the author's father-in-law, Henry Honda, who was 23 at the time, and a ball player.

Manoa resident Jane Okubo says her father, Hideo "Kuro" Yoshiyama, played for the Waiakea Pirates that day. "He had a ball signed by him, and kept a big picture of Ruth and the Waiakea Pirates under glass on a coffee table for 50 years. Playing with Babe Ruth was one of the high points of his life."

Which famous musical group began at Punahou School?

The biggest musical group to ever come out of Hawaii was the Kingston Trio. Honolulu Advertiser photos.

THIS THREE-SOME LAUNCHED an interest in folk music and paved the way for such artists as Peter, Paul & Mary and Bob Dylan. The group was the Kingston Trio, arguably the biggest group to come out of Hawaii. The Trio became the No. 1 vocal group in the world until the Beatles came along.

Two of the trio, Dave Guard and Bob Shane went to Punahou School together and graduated in 1952. In their junior year they formed a group to sing at the Punahou Carnival, performing songs by the Weavers, the most popular folk group of the time.

Shane was from Hilo and took up the guitar to gain some popularity with girls. Guard was from Waikiki and his idol was Gabby Pahinui. "When my folks gave me my earliest guitar," Guard recalled, "I learned to play in the G slack key tuning first."

"I would hang around the Queen's Surf night club just to hear Gabby's trio (with Joe Diamond and Ralph Alapai.) I pestered Gabby for lessons and he showed me one of

Gabby Pahinui was an inspiration to Kingston Trio member Bob Shane..

his C tunings, but he said 'It's not how you tune' em up, it's how you pluck 'em.' "

After graduation, the two went to Bay Area colleges. Shane formed a duet with Nick Reynolds, a college buddy. The duo sang at parties, school functions, and occasionally, Dave joined them as a trio. They took the capital of Jamaica, — Kingston — as their name because they saw themselves as a Calypso group.

In February 1958, the group recorded its first album entitled simply *The Kingston Trio*. The record included the songs *Scotch and Soda*, and *Tom Dooley*. It sold more than 3,000,000 copies and earned them a Grammy. Both Billboard and Cash Box magazines voted the trio The Best Group Of The Year in 1959.

Most listeners did not know that the richness of the Trio's harmonies was the result of a double-voicing recording technique. During the first take, the voices were recorded softer than the

guitars and banjo. Then they'd over-dub the singing, creating a six-voice choral effect. This process would often take 50-100 takes to get it right.

The Kingston Trio's other hits included *Greenback Dollar, MTA, Tijuana Jail, Worried Man,* and *Wreck of the John B,* which was later covered by the Beach Boys. The group had five albums on the Billboard Top Ten at one time, and inspired hundreds of folk groups all over the country, notably Peter, Paul & Mary, The Brothers Four, The Chad Mitchell Trio, The Limeliters, and The New Christy Minstrels.

—*Researched by Lizzy Lynch*

Dave Guard, left, and Bob Shane, right, met at Punahou School. They joined Nick Reynolds, center, in California.

Which restaurant is gone but its salad dressing remains?

The Tropics Restaurant occupied the site that is now the Ala Moana Hotel. Honolulu Advertiser *photo.*

ONE OF HAWAII'S FAVORITE SALAD DRESSINGS — Tropics — began as a restaurant.

Tony and Peaches Gurerro retired from Hollywood movies and opened the Tropics Restaurant in Waikiki in 1940.

Soon they had three. One on Kalakaua where Macy's is today. One where the Ala Moana Hotel is, and the third was in Hilo.

Their french salad dressing was so popular that patrons would bring in containers and want to buy some. The Guererro's didn't know what to charge for so many different size containers, so they started bottling it themselves. The restaurants closed in 1968.

Which hotel has had a fire burning in its fireplace since 1888?

When Volcano House burned down in 1940, staff rescued the fire.

O NE of our hotels has had a fire burning in its fireplace for almost 120 continuous years. It's the oldest hotel in the islands. It sits on the site of Hawaii's first tourist destination. Can you name it?

It's Volcano House. A fire was begun in 1888 and has been kept continuously burning since then.

Even when the hotel burned down in 1940, the staff rescued embers from the fireplace and kept them burning in the Volcano Museum until the Volcano House was rebuilt, The embers were then carefully transferred back to the new fireplace.

Volcano House first opened in 1865 as the Crater Hotel.

Mark Twain stayed at the hotel and was mesmerized by the volcanic fountains. His writings spurred a tourism boom to the Big Island.

A fire has burned in the Volcano House fireplace since 1888. Honolulu Advertiser *photos.*

The first Iolani Palace

DID you know that there was an earlier Iolani Palace? The palace we have today was built by King Kalakaua in 1882.

The original Iolani Palace was a modest, one story coral block house.

The original palace was built during the reign of Alexander Liholiho Iolani, King Kamehameha IV in 1844, who relocated from Lahaina to be closer to whalers and merchants in Honolulu.

The one-story, coral block building was the official residence of four monarchs: Kamehameha IV, Kamehameha V, Lunalilo, and Kalakaua.

King Kalakaua was elected in 1873. He was inspired by the palaces he saw on his 1881 "around the world tour." While on his tour, Kalakaua met with Thomas Edison and asked him to help bring electricity to Hawaii. Kalakaua replaced the original palace, which suffered from termite damage, with one befitting a modern state, such as Hawaii in 1882.

Four years later, in 1886, Edison sent someone to electrify Iolani Palace. It took the White House another four years to have electricity. Iolani Palace was the first royal palace in the world to have electricity.

Which sports legend played football in Hawaii in 1941 before breaking baseball's color barrier?

Jackie Robinson, right, played semi-pro football in Hawaii in 1941. Honolulu Advertiser *photos.*

H E WAS THE FIRST UCLA Bruin to letter in four different sports — baseball, football, basketball, and track. He came to Hawaii on the *Matsonia* in 1941 and lived in Kaimuki. Who was he?

Jackie Robinson is well-known for being the first African American to play in major league baseball. But did you know that he lived and played semi-pro football in Hawaii six years earlier?

Robinson was a celebrity when he arrived in Hawaii. A full-length picture ran in the *Honolulu Advertiser* with an invitation to "See the sensational, all-American half-back, Jackie Robinson."

The Honolulu Bears, (formerly the Honolulu Polar Bears!) of the semiprofessional Hawaii Senior Football League, offered him $100 a game (about $1,000 in 2008 dollars) as well as a job in construction during the day at Pearl Harbor.

Robinson moved into a duplex apartment in Kaimuki near Saint Louis College. A record crowd of 20,000 came to see his first game, which the Honolulu Bears lost to the Healani Maroons.

"Robinson reeled off some brilliant runs," the newspaper said,

Former Honolulu resident, Jackie Robinson, became the first African American to play in major league baseball in 1947.

"but faltered in his passing, many of his attempts being intercepted." By the end of the season in December, Robinson was injured, the Bears fared poorly and the crowd dwindled to less than 600.

Jackie Robinson was discouraged and homesick. He left Hawaii on the *Lurline* on December 5, 1941. Two days later, the captain called the passengers together and notified them of the attack on Pearl Harbor. The ship would sail with the portholes blacked out, and would slip in and out of sea lanes to avoid possible submarines.

Following World War II in 1945, Los Angeles Dodger owner Branch Rickey wanted to integrate baseball. This was still three years before the armed forces were integrated, and nine years before segregation was outlawed in public schools.

In April of 1947, Robinson donned a Dodger uniform and became the first African American in major league baseball. And this heroic act was done by someone who once lived in Hawaii.

Which Honolulu street's name means "house of God" in Hebrew?

"BETH" MEANS HOUSE in Hebrew. "El" is God. The street was named for the Seaman's Bethel, a church built near the waterfront in 1833 by the American Seamen's Friend Society to minister to English-speaking sailors from whaling and trading ships. Samuel Damon came to Hawaii to lead the church, which provided an alternative to bars and saloons.

In 1852, some local parishioners formed the Fort Street Church, on the corner of Fort and Beretania, where HPU is today. The church founded Hawaii's first public high school in 1865. This English Day School eventually became McKinley High School.

After a waterfront fire destroyed the Seamen's Bethel in 1886,

the two congregations merged to form Central Union Church on Richards Street, on the grounds of what is now the State Capitol.

The growing parish needed more space, and moved in 1924 to "Woodlawn," the former Dillingham estate on Beretania and Punahou streets. So, today, the church built for whalers has evolved into Central Union Church.

Parishioners of the church have launched many other churches, organizations, and schools, including: McKinley High School, Princess Kaiulani Elementary School, La Pietra — Hawaii School for Girls, the Honolulu Boy Choir, Arcadia Retirement Residence, Palama Settlement, the First Chinese Church of Christ, and Makiki Christian Church.

Left: Seaman's Bethel Chapel, from an 1843 woodcut published in "The Friend." Hawaii State Archives photos. Below: Central Union Church along with dozens of other churches and schools grew out of the Seaman's Bethel.

Which festival, begun in 1964, once featured barbershop quartets, beard contests, beer drinking, and hula?

HERE'S A CLUE: IT WAS HELD AT HILO'S CIVIC Auditorium, but only about 300 people attended.

If you guessed the Merrie Monarch Festival, you would be right. The "Olympics of Hula" we know today began very humbly as a way to stimulate the economy after the 1960 Hilo tsunami. It was organized by the Chamber of Commerce, and its theme was the royal-court pageantry of King Kalakaua and the Gay Nineties.

The festival was a flop. The Chamber wanted to discontinue it but Dottie Thompson stepped in. She didn't want to lose another Hawaiian festival, so she called in Albert Nahalea, of the Hawaiian Homelands Department, and hula master George Naope and they brainstormed.

Naope suggested honoring King Kalakaua, who was called the Merrie Monarch, with dancers from all over the kingdom. In 1969 and 1970 the festival was a recreation of his coronation.

Kumu hula Pauline Kekahuna and Louise Kaleiki then suggested the following year's focus be on a hula competition. The one-night event was first held in 1971 and included modern hula. Kahiko, or ancient hula, was added in 1972. KITV began covering the festival in 1981.

In 1996, Dottie Thompson was named a Living Legend by the County of Hawaii Department of Parks and Recreation for her role in preserving the art of hula and the Hawaiian culture.

In a recent interview, Naope, who has danced the hula for over 70 years, said people tell him he's great. "Shee. Every morning when

I wake up, I go to the lua, and look at the mirror and I go 'Mirror, mirror on the wall, who's the greatest of them all?' And you know, that s.o.b. never answer yet. So that means I not great. And if it did answer, I wouldn't be here. I would die of a heart attack!"

The early festivals were held at the Hilo Civic Auditorium. By 1979, they needed more room and moved to the Edith Kanaka'ole Stadium. "Auntie Edith" was one of Hawaii's most revered kumu hula. She came from a long family tradition of hula, and was an instructor of Hawaiian studies at Hawaii Community College and the U.H.-Hilo. Gov. George Ariyoshi awarded Kanaka'ole with an Order of Distinction for Cultural Leadership.

The Merrie Monarch Festival began in 1964 as a way to help Hilo recover from the 1960 tsunami. King David Kalakaua was called the Merrie Monarch. Honolulu Advertiser *photo.*

How Christmas came to the islands

MANY ASSUME THE MISSIONARIES BROUGHT
Christmas to the islands, but they did not celebrate it
since it's not mentioned in the Bible. Here's a look at
how Christmas really came to Hawaii.

King Kamehameha IV witnessed Christmas festivities in England as a young man, and is largely responsible for making Christmas an official holiday in Hawaii. Right: Nathaniel Portlock exchanged Hawaii's first Christmas gifts in 1819.

While the Puritans did not celebrate Christmas, the English did. An English ship, the *Charlotte*, happened to be exploring Waimea Bay, Kauai on Christmas day, 1786. Captain George Dixon had a pig roasted. The crew made pies, and grog was mixed with coconut milk. The crew toasted friends and family at home in England, and the miles between the two island kingdoms were bridged for a moment. It was Hawaii's first Christmas dinner.

Hawaii's first Christmas gifts were exchanged in 1819. Capt. Nathaniel Portlock (right) noted in his log that chief "Kiana came off a double canoe and brought me a present of some hogs and vegetables, which I received gladly, and prepared in return, and that pleased him very much."

In New England, the first missionaries set sail for Hawaii aboard the *Thaddeus* in 1819. Since the Bible doesn't mention Christmas, the Puritans did not observe it. Christianity, but not Christmas, was on its way to Hawaii.

Catholics first came to Hawaii in 1826 and did celebrate Christmas. Their spirit infected the missionary wives, who, by 1837, began to join the festivities. They made quiet shopping trips to town and talked about what they should cook and whom they should invite to the coming holiday dinner.

Prince Alexander Liholiho, who would later become Kamehameha IV, was a nine-year-old student at the Chiefs' Children's School in 1843. He led a revolt against studying on Christmas Day. Schoolmaster Amos Cooke wrote that "the children thought it would be doing God's work to devote this day to merriment. The girls baked cakes and the boys made candy, and all are making ready presents for Christmas."

Hawaii's first Christmas Tree made its appearance at Washington Place in the 1850s.

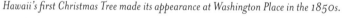

By 1856, Kamehameha IV, who had witnessed the great festival of Christmas in Europe, set aside December 25, 1856, as a national day of Thanksgiving!

In the next few years, Christmas toys and decorations became plentiful in the stores.

Mary Dominis threw a Christmas Eve party at Washington Place in 1858. Hawaii's first Christmas tree made its appearance, and there were party favors. Bells were heard at the windows announcing Hawaii's first Santa Claus with gifts for everyone.

On December 25, 1862, Christmas was proclaimed a holiday in Hawaii by the authority of King Kamehameha IV.

The city threw itself into the preparations. Churches throughout the land threw spectacular celebrations. In the newspapers, merchants advertised "toys in great supply and dolls of all kinds," and Christmas displays were put up in stores.

On Christmas Eve, the Catholic Cathedral of Our Lady Of Peace was illuminated with wreaths of light. Inside, the altars were beautifully decorated and more than a thousand candles were lit.

The tree at the Fort Street Church carried more than 200 small lights and its branches were burdened with gifts for more than 70 students, with no two gifts alike.

After the Midnight Christmas services concluded, the Punchbowl gun batteries were fired. The King and the Bishop began their slow procession from St. Andrews church to the Palace. Twenty torch bearers lit the way for the members of the congregation and the choir.

The procession marched in slow cadence through the streets of Honolulu, singing Christmas carols. Christmas had come to Hawaii.

Ala Moana Center's Grand Opening

EVERYONE SHOPS AT ALA MOANA, but that wasn't always so. Local retailers actually considered it a huge risk to move from downtown, and what had been Hawaii's main shopping area for well over 100 years.

Back in the 1950s, Ala Moana was swamp land. A wave of middle class tourism was just beginning to crash over Waikiki. Locals flocked downtown to shop at Liberty House, McInerny, Kramer's, Carol & Mary, Ming's, Ethel's, Andrade, Kress and the Ritz.

Former *Honolulu Advertiser* editor Bud Smyser recalled "the alarm in the downtown business community on learning that a giant shopping center was planned for the Dillingham property between downtown and Waikiki. Downtowners feared it could decimate downtown retailing."

Two aerial views of Ala Moana Center's grand opening. Over 1,000 people came out on August 13, 1959, to the roof deck outside Longs and Sears. The crowd of 1,000 is a fuzzy patch on the right, upper parking deck..

Small stores were unsure customers would follow them if they left downtown for the new center. However, when Sears agreed to be the anchor tenant, it paved the way for smaller stores to follow. If a giant like Sears could do it, they felt they could take the chance too.

One week before the territory became a state on August 21, 1959 Ala Moana Center held its grand opening. Phase I was the Ewa wing of the center. It opened on August 13. A crowd of over 1,000 stood on the upper parking deck, outside Longs.

Walter Dillingham and his son Lowell, Governor William Quinn and Mayor Neal S. Blaisdell welcomed the crowd. King Kalakaua was hailed as Hawaii's first "merchant king." Musical and hula groups performed on three stages.

The Grand Opening ceremonies can be seen at the far left, ouside Longs. Honolulu Advertiser *photos.*

The open-air mall had two levels and encompassed 680,000 leasable square feet of space. A two-level parking deck could accommodate over 4,000 cars. It cost only $25 million to build, and 87 tenants moved in, including Shirokiya, Sears, Longs, Foodland, Woolworth, Slipper House, HOPACO, Carol & Mary, McInerny, Pocketbook Man, Ming's and Iida's. By several measures, it was the largest shopping center in the world.

Walter Dillingham purchased the 50 acres of what was then swampland in 1912 for $25,000 ($500,000 today) figuring "it might be useful someday." For 35 years, it sat, used for nothing but a place for coral dredged out of Honolulu Harbor. Soon after World War II, in 1948, Dillingham said he started thinking about a shopping center.

Donald Graham, a VP at the Hawaiian Land Company, a subsidiary of Hawaiian Dredging, took the lead in its design. His "pride and joy" was a signature revolving cocktail lounge. It first showed up in design plans in 1952 — in the middle of the shopping center. "We moved it all over the place," Graham recalls, before finally placing it atop the Ala Moana building on the mauka side of the center.

La Ronde was Hawaii's first rotating restaurant in 1961. The Top of Waikiki was second in 1965 and is still open.

Phase II of the center opened in 1966. The three-level addition was anchored by a 245,000 square foot Liberty House store. J.C. Penney moved into an 180,000 square foot space and Shirokiya relocated into 53,000 square feet.

General Growth Partners bought the center in 1999 for $810 million. Today, Ala Moana Center is the world's largest outdoor shopping center with 190 stores and 70 restaurants, occupying 2 million square feet. Annual sales top $1 billion.

Five of Ala Moana Center's original tenants can still be found there: Slipper House, Shirokiya, Longs, Sears, and Foodland. Slipper House was founded in 1952 by Florence Kamimoto and Kiyoto Uejio. They formerly had a store on Hotel Street, near Fort, and another on Young Street, near Kalakaua. On opening day at Ala Moana Center in 1959, they gave away 500 pairs of slippers, causing a mob scene.

Walter and Lowell Dillingham and a man representing King Kalakaua at Ala Moana Center's grand opening in 1959. Note a young Hal "Aku" Lewis, wearing sunglasses, in the lower left, covering the event for KHVH radio.

The Ilikai Hotel

WHEN IT OPENED IN 1964, the Ilikai was the largest condominium in the world. It was a testament to the tenacity of Chinn Ho, who built it on what had once been his parents' rice field and duck ponds.

Ho was a McKinley high school graduate and became president of the Hawaii Visitors Bureau, owned the *Honolulu Star-Bulletin*, the Hawaii Islanders baseball team, as well as his own company, Capital Investment. Chinn Ho's success was an inspiration to many Asian Americans who had previously been held back by a racial divide that eroded after World War II.

The hit TV show, *Hawaii Five-O*, showed Jack Lord atop the Ilikai in its opening sequence, publicizing the hotel to millions. And a character in the show was named Chin Ho Kelley. Ilikai means the "surface of the sea."

—*Researched by Remy Cremers*

Below: Chinn Ho's model of his plans for the Ilikai in 1961 was the largest, most intricate ever made in Hawaii. It weighed 500 pounds. Left: Under construction in 1963. Honolulu Advertiser *photos.*

The Wallabies of Kalihi Valley

Y OU'VE HEARD ABOUT THEM, but do the wallabies really exist? The answer is yes, and they've inhabited the back of Kalihi Valley for over 90 years.

When Alewa Heights was being built in 1916, the developer was looking for something to attract attention to his new homes. He brought in three wallabies from a visiting circus for a private zoo. But before he could build it, neighborhood dogs attacked the tent the wallabies were residing in and they escaped.

Zoo Director Paul Breese shows off Wally the Wallaby, captured in Kalihi Valley in 1954. Honolulu Advertiser *photos.*

The wallabies established colonies that ranged from Halawa to Nuuanu valleys, but an increase in development squeezed them to just one colony of 40-200 members in the back of Kalihi Valley.

However, they are known to wander. In 2002, the Tabalanza family of Foster Village found one eating grass in their backyard. The Humane Society returned him to Kalihi Valley after a check-up.

The Brush-tailed Rock Wallaby is different from all remaining species of Australian wallabies. It has adapted to eating Hawaiian plants that would be poisonous to its relatives down-under.

Many recall seeing Jack Lord around town, dressed in white, as in this 1980 Honolulu Advertiser photo.

The day Jack Lord was almost Fired From Hawaii Five-O

Jack Lord was almost fired by "Hawaii Five-O" producer Leonard Freeman, below, who planned to replace him with Lloyd Bridges. Honolulu Advertiser *photos.*

I T'S HARD TO IMAGINE, but Jack Lord was nearly fired by *Hawaii Five-O* producer Leonard Freeman.

Former *Honolulu Advertiser* columnist Eddie Sherman, in his book, *Frank, Sammy, Marlon, & Me,* relates how Freeman was offered stock in the ownership of the sound stage that *Hawaii Five-O* used — a potential conflict of interest. Sherman was president of the company that owned the sound stage.

Jack Lord found out about the stock and informed CBS. Freeman was able to explain the situation to them, but was furious with Jack Lord. Freeman told CBS "his first order of business upon landing would be to visit Jack Lord and fire him. I don't need the star of my show stabbing me in the back," he said.

Leonard Freeman told Eddie Sherman that Jack Lord's replacement would be Lloyd Bridges! Jack Lord became hysterical. He explained he didn't intend to get Freeman in

Oops! An explosion during "Hawaii Five-O" filming accidentally blew out windows at several storefronts.

trouble. Lord then got on the floor and grabbed Freeman around the ankles and begged for forgiveness.

"Have you ever seen a grown man cry?" Freeman asked Eddie Sherman. "I just couldn't fire him."

Additionally, there are a few more tidbits you probably didn't know about *Hawaii Five-O*. The idea for the show came from Freeman's mother-in-law, who used to live in Hawaii, and encouraged him to produce a show here.

Jack Lord was seriously considered for the role of Captain Kirk in *Star Trek*. Lord wanted to co-produce the series and own a percentage of it. The show's creator, Gene Roddenberry wasn't willing to meet his demands and cast William Shatner instead.

This composite picture shows what Jack Lord would look like had he been cast in Star Trek.

Japan's Pearl Harbor Miscalculation

Admiral Isoroku Yamamoto. Official portrait, by Shugaku Homma, 1943. U.S. Naval Historical Center photograph.

JAPAN MADE A STRATEGIC error in attacking Pearl Harbor that allowed the U.S. to rebound quickly and eventually defeat them. This error also shortened the war in Europe, and may have prevented the use of nuclear weapons there. What was that error?

The Japanese attack destroyed or severely damaged 188 aircraft, five battleships, three destroyers, and took 2,403 lives. However, Pearl Harbor's dry docks were relatively unscathed by the first two waves of Japanese planes.

Many of the Japanese pilots expected they would re-fuel and re-arm after the initial two waves at Pearl Harbor and return to attack dockyard installations, and ship repair and maintenance facilities in a third wave. Without this infrastructure, rebuilding the U.S. Pacific Fleet would have been more difficult.

The Pearl Harbor fuel reserves were also largely untouched by the initial attack. The Japanese did this to prevent smoke from obscuring our ships. A planned third wave targeted them.

U.S. fuel reserves turned out to be essential to our success later in the war. Some historians believe the elimination of those fuel tanks and repair facilities would have hurt the Pacific Fleet more than the loss of battleships.

Additionally, the submarine base at Pearl Harbor had only minimal damage. The U.S. submarine fleet went on to sink over 50% of Japanese ships in the next three years.

Japan estimated the U.S. Pacific Fleet would be put out of action for six months, but instead we were engaging them in a matter of weeks. Six months after Pearl Harbor, the U.S. Navy defeated the Japanese Fleet at Midway, marking the turning point of the war.

Vice Admiral Nagumo called off a planned Third Wave attack, believing they had accomplished all their objectives.

Vice Admiral Nagumo believed that all of their Pearl Harbor objectives had been met. Commander-in-Chief Admiral Yamamoto's main intent was to keep the U.S. from interfering with Japan's Southeast Asian invasion. The main objective was securing oil and other natural resources from the Dutch East Indies.

Nagumo believed his main task at that point was to return his six aircraft carriers, the only ones Japan possessed, safely home, for their next missions.

By coincidence, the carriers *Enterprise, Saratoga* and *Lexington* were hundreds of miles west of Kauai at the time of the attack. However, it was the survival of our shipyard repair facilities that allowed us to quickly get back in the game.

The Battle of Midway

Admiral Chester A. Nimitz led our forces in recovering from Pearl Harbor. In less than 6 months, the tide turned at the Battle of Midway in our favor. Honolulu Advertiser *photos.*

One of the world's foremost authorities on the Battle of Midway is a Kailua man named Alan Lloyd. "The first Japanese mistake at Pearl Harbor was that they left our dry-docks and shipyards intact, and concentrated on sinking ships. But we were able to refloat and repair many ships quickly," Lloyd says.

The aircraft carrier *Yorktown* was badly damaged at the battle of the Coral Seas and limped back to Pearl Harbor. It was estimated to take months to repair. "Nimitz demanded it sail in 48 hours," Lloyd says "and it left for Midway two days later with six of nine boilers working."

"After Pearl Harbor, Japan felt they could run wild in the Pacific. Their intentions at Midway were to draw out our Pacific Fleet and sink our carriers."

"But they lost one of their six carriers, the *Shokaku*, at Coral Seas, and another, the *Zuikaku*, lost most of its airplanes," Lloyd continues. "Both had to sit out Midway. That was their second mistake. They didn't concentrate their resources like Admiral Nimitz did."

We were able to have 4 carriers — the *Yorktown, Hornet, Enterprise* and *Saratoga* — at Midway because Pearl's dry docks were operational.

"The Japanese thought they'd take us by surprise at Midway, Lloyd continues. "But our naval intelligence units at Hickam, led by Joe Rochefort, broke their code. He predicted the Japanese would be at 325 degrees west longitude, 180 miles off Midway and attack at 6 AM,

174

on June 4, 1942. He was off by 5 degrees, 5 miles and 30 minutes. It was our greatest naval intelligence victory. Rochefort was really the unsung hero of the battle."

Adm. Nimitz surprised the Japanese at Midway and sunk four of her six fleet carriers. "Imagine how the battle might have gone, if the Japanese had the carrier *Zuikaku*, and we didn't have the *Yorktown*," Lloyd muses.

Naval Intelligence officer Joe Rochefort was the unsung hero of the Battle of Midway.

The outcome of the battle affected the war in Europe. "If we had lost Midway, European resources would have had to be deployed to the Pacific," Lloyd believes. "D-day could not have occurred on June 6, 1944. The U.S. might have felt compelled to use nuclear weapons in Europe."

Thus a minor change in Japanese tactics at Pearl Harbor affected the Battle of Midway and the whole outcome of the war.

The Battle of Taranto

Few seem to know that the attack on Pearl Harbor was inspired by the Battle of Taranto in Italy on November 11, 1940. In *Operation Judgement*, the British launched 20 obsolete biplane bombers from aircraft carriers. It was the first time that planes alone carried out a naval attack, but it disabled half of the Italian fleet. The remaining Italian Navy retreated to northern bases.

A Japanese naval delegation to Italy felt that a similar attack could force the U.S. Pacific Fleet to retreat to bases in California. They based their Pearl Harbor plans on this little-known Italian battle.

The Wackiest Ship in the Army

MANY BABY BOOMERS IN HAWAII might remember the 1960 movie of the same name that starred Jack Lemmon and a young Ricky Nelson.

But few of them might know it was a true story and the ship's captain is a Hawaii Kai resident.

The captain was Meredith "Rip" Riddle. During World War II he was given the assignment to drop "coast watchers" to observe Japanese ship movements in the South Pacific. The order came from General MacArthur himself.

World War II buffs know that the war was largely won because of superior military intelligence. The U.S. broke both the Japanese and German codes and could read their communications. Part of this effort was to place coast watchers on South Pacific islands to observe Japanese ships, and radio their whereabouts.

In the movie, one of these coast watchers had been killed and the Army desperately needed to replace him. They conscripted an old schooner, the *Echo*, to slip through enemy waters and deliver the Australian coast watchers. Captain Rip Crandall (as they called him in the movie) had been a yachtsman and was given the assignment.

To fool Japanese ships and scout planes, several crewmembers wore grass skirts, wigs and coconut bras to appear to be native women. "We were followed by the enemy but managed to avoid them," Riddle says. "We sailed out in the open and they believed we were innocent and left us alone."

The 1960 movie, "The Wackiest Ship in the Army," seen filming here at Pearl Harbor, was based on the real-life adventures of Hawaii Kai resident Rip Riddle. Honolulu Advertiser *photos.*

The *Echo* succeeded in its mission and the information the scouts provided was crucial in winning several South Pacific battles.

"The movie oversimplified what we did," Riddle believes. "Thousands of coast watchers — they didn't like to be called 'spies' — helped in the war effort all over the South Pacific. We dropped off only one in the movie, but in actuality, it was probably around 50."

Riddle says they did wear coconut bras and grass skirts a few times,

but the ship was never captured or sunk, as in the movie. Instead, it was returned to its Wellington, New Zealand owners.

Riddle did have a young executive officer as played by Ricky Nelson in the movie, named Bob Shannon. "The entire 12 man crew was outstanding, and deserves all the credit," Riddle says.

Readers may have been intrigued by the title — shouldn't it have been *The Wackiest Ship in the Navy*? "We were loaned to the Army and took orders from them," Riddle explains, "But remained under the final guidance of the Navy."

Riddle was very pleased with the small part he says he played in the war effort and is happy he managed to get through it. However, he credits thousands of others who did their share and doesn't want to be seen as a hero. "There were a lot of people helping."

Some of his work was humanitarian. "We had tons of SPAM and

Left: Jack Lemmon and Ricky Nelson, starred in the film.
Above: Hawaii Kai resident Meredith "Rip" Riddle was the real life captain of the Echo..

corned beef, and gave a lot of it to natives who were hungry. We managed to do pretty good at helping out."

Was he afraid, we asked? "You can't say you're not scared. But you can't live with your heart in your mouth and be normal. Maybe that's why I'm not normal!"

Admiral Nimitz came to meet the crew when they returned to Pearl Harbor. "He met everyone coming back," Riddle recalls, "congratulating them and thanking them for what they did. He was a quiet old gent, reminded me more like my grandfather than a fleet admiral. But he was a sharp guy and knew his business. I was with him on several occasions and liked him very much."

After the war, Riddle wrote up his story for *Argosy* magazine. It was turned into a movie and a short-lived TV show. The movie was filmed at Pearl Harbor, and the South Pacific Island of New Britain, which has an uncanny resemblance to Waimea Canyon and Opaekaa Falls on Kauai.

Hollywood jumped into the World War II genre in the 1950s with a set of mostly non-combat war comedies about leaky ships with oddball crews. *Mister Roberts* (1955), *South Pacific* (1958), and *Operation Petticoat* (1959), paved the way for *The Wackiest Ship in the Army* (1960), which in turn led to the hit TV show *McHale's Navy* (1962-66).

Riddle worked in the Hawaii maritime business after the war and has lived here for 45 years. He's spent the last three years writing his memoirs, called *My Four Seasons*.

Funny moments on early, local TV news

Wayne Collins was Hawaii's first news anchor in the mid-1950s. Honolulu Advertiser *photo.*

IN HONOLULU in the early 1950s, the Pan American World News was the only TV newscast on the only TV channel in Hawaii. Wayne Collins was the first news anchor.

"Most of the 15 minute show was my talking head on camera," Collins recalls, "although we had a few kinescope film-clips from the West Coast on a 1- or 2-day delay. We had no camera man nor processing capability. Our lead local story usually featured a live interview, with the guest shoe-horned in behind the news desk with me."

The commercials usually consisted of silent film clips or still photos. "During the early days we had no slide projectors, so stills and any text had to be mounted on posters by a staff artist and placed on easels on the set. Floor cameras were simply pointed at them, and any text superimposed by the chaps in the control room."

The news sponsor had a model Pan American airliner suspended in midair by black threads in front of a rotating world globe. The globe was about the size of a soccer ball, mounted atop a waist-high pillar. To give the shot a sense of movement, the floor camera with a big zoom lens was used, and would zoom in slowly to a close-up of the plane and globe.

One evening as that particular shot began, the zoom lens had not been "pulled back" so it could not zoom in. "But the director in the control room wanted the customary inward movement and instructed the camera-man forcefully and repeatedly to 'dolly in, dolly in tighter!' He did as he was told, not noticing how close he was to the suspended model and the rotating globe."

Sure enough, the hydraulic base of the camera crashed into the pedestal. "The earth quivered, touched the model and then toppled," Collins remembers. "To the viewer, the world fell out of sight with a crash and a bang."

The globe's electric motor shorted out and exploded when it hit the polished concrete floor. A rising spiral of smoke engulfed the jittery Pan American airliner.

"The airliner jiggled in the smoke, shouts were heard in the background, the control room was chaos, the voice-over droned on about 'the world's most experienced airline,' somebody finally cut to another floor camera and a shot of a bemused newscaster trying hard not to grin. I doubt I was successful."

Which Hawaii nonprofit considered moving to the Cheyenne River Sioux Indian Reservation in South Dakota?

IN 1995, HAWAII'S LARGEST CHARITABLE TRUST considered moving to South Dakota. Why? To avoid the scrutiny of the IRS and state government. Which organization would ever consider doing such a thing?

The answer is the former trustees of the Kamehameha Schools/ Bishop Estate — Henry Peters, Dickie Wong, Lokelani Lindsay, Gerard Jervis and Oswald Stender. They hired former Governor Waihee's Washington D.C. law firm to review the legal and tax consequences of relocating out of Hawaii.

The $300,000 fee got them a confidential, thirty page report that recommended the ideal environment for the trust was the Cheyenne River Sioux Indian Reservation, 50 miles northwest of South Dakota's capital, Pierre.

It wasn't the rolling prairie, rivers, and creeks they found attractive. It was the autonomy from the federal government and the exemption from paying federal taxes that the trustees wanted. According to the state's former attorney general, Margery Bronster, "their main motivation was to avoid oversight from the state attorney general and the IRS."

Bronster was investigating the trustees. She found the estate was neglecting their duty to the children of Hawaii by engaging in cronyism, corruption, and abuse of power.

These abuses were detailed in a 1997 series of articles published in the *Honolulu Star-Bulletin* entitled *Broken Trust*, authored by Gladys Brandt, Msgr. Charles Kekumano, Walter Heen, Samuel King, and Randall Roth The 6,400-word essay charged that "underqualified and overpaid trustees had been selected in a rigged political process, had engaged in loose and self-serving financial management and had distinguished themselves mostly by conflicts of interest, disdain for accountability, greed and arrogance."

Broken Trust set off a firestorm of protest in the community and was covered by *60 Minutes, the Wall Street Journal, USA Today, New York Times,* and *the Washington Post.* It was "the biggest news story to hit Hawaii since Pearl Harbor," said former *Honolulu Advertiser* editor George Chaplain.

Former Gov. John Waihee's law firm was hired by the Bishop Estate to recommend other states where they would have less government oversight. Honolulu Advertiser *photo*

State and federal investigations were launched and Hawaiians were shocked at their findings. Many feared the tax-exempt status of the estate was in jeopardy, which could cost the estate $750 million. This realization motivated the trustees to consider becoming a for-profit entity and moving to a Native American reservation where they would be free from scrutiny.

In May of 1999, Oswald Stender resigned and the court removed the other four trustees from their offices. The new trustees lowered their compensation from over $1 million per year to a more modest $90,000. The citizens of Honolulu breathed a collective sigh of relief.

Which infamous assassin's brother was once an actor in Honolulu?

THE ASSASSIN WAS JOHN WILKES BOOTH. His brother, Edwin Thomas Booth was an actor on the verge of national fame when his younger sibling killed President Abraham Lincoln.

The two brothers were actors, as was their father, Junius. Ironically, John Wilkes Booth shot Lincoln in a theatre — Ford's.

The story is also ironic in that Abraham Lincoln's son, Robert was saved from serious injury or even death by Edwin Booth in New Jersey after Robert had fallen onto a train platform.

Edwin Booth was born in Maryland in 1833. When he was 21, he traveled to Australia, where he acted briefly in Sydney and Melbourne.

He and several others then came to Hawaii where they rented the Royal Hawaiian Theatre for $50. They hired young boys to paste up flyers for Shakespeare's *Richard III*.

The actress playing Lady Anne argued with Booth and stormed off. A stagehand had to replace her. To make matters worse, he was a cross-eyed and bow-legged man with two front teeth missing. Make up and a dress didn't seem to help, and certainly didn't come close to Shakespeare's words: "Divine perfection of a woman."

The other actors couldn't contain their laughter off-stage, but the audience enjoyed the evening.

King Kamehameha IV attended one of their first performances in March 1855, but because his father had recently died, the king could not appear publicly.

The King was provided a chair in the wings, but he had to relinquish it when it had to be used as a throne in the play. His majesty graciously got up and watched standing.

He told Booth later that he enjoyed the play, and patted him on the back. As a young man, the King told him, he had traveled to New York and had seen his father, Junius, play *Richard III*.

Booth and his fellow actors made enough money to book passage to California and his brief stay in Hawaii was over. Booth received substantial acclaim for his acting later that

Edwin Booth, the brother of assassin John Wilkes Booth, was briefly an actor in Hawaii.

year in California and New York.

The 1865 assassination of the president by his brother blackened his name and caused him to retire from the theatre, but within a year, he returned and performed until 1891. Upon his death, two years later, some theatre historians called him the greatest American actor of the 19th century.

The Royal Hawaiian Theatre was the second in Hawaii, after the Thespian (at King and Maunakea Streets), which opened in 1847. The Royal Hawaiian Theatre opened in 1848 at Hotel and Alakea Streets, where the courthouse now stands. Shaped like a Quonset hut, it sat 200 people.

A hotel was built on the same block in 1871. It was originally named the Hawaiian Hotel, but the named soon became the Royal Hawaiian Hotel, possibly because of its next door neighbor. Matson bought the name in 1917 and used it for his Waikiki hotel, which opened in 1927.

Hawaii's one and only Great Train Robbery

W E ONCE HAD TRAINS ON SEVERAL ISLANDS. Passengers and goods were transported for two decades from the plantations to town before the first cars and trucks appeared in Hawaii. And even then, it took 50 years for cars to displace trains in the late 1940s.

However, only one of those trains was ever robbed. It happened in 1920 by a man who apparently watched too many western movies. And it took place in one of the unlikeliest of places — Kekaha, Kauai.

Only one train robbery has occurred in Hawaii, in Kekaha, Kauai in 1920. The robber, Kaimiola Hali, had watched too many western movies. He was caught the following day. Bishop Museum photo.

The locomotives on Kauai were small and slow moving. The payroll for the plantation was $13,000 in gold and silver coins.

Around 5 PM on February 11, 1920, the train was rounding a curve in the line, when a masked man boarded the locomotive with a pistol. He took possession of the strongbox and ordered the paymaster and engineer off the train, where he had them uncouple the locomotive from the passenger car.

Kaimiola Hali had watched the train for months and dreamed. "I think I can; I think I can rob that train," he must have thought. He drove the locomotive to a fork in the line and took the mauka track, not knowing an empty cane car awaited up the line.

Hali pushed the cane car for a while, but then threw the strongbox off the train, put it in reverse and jumped off. The train slowly retraced its steps until it reached the engineer who had been robbed. They quickly realized that the cane car marked the forward position of the robber.

The sheriff found the now-empty strongbox and the robbers mask nearby. Hali joined in looking for the robber, but acted strangely and caused suspicion to fall on himself. Neighbors said Hali had once worked on a train and knew how to operate it. Still another said the fisherman liked to watch western movies. Hali was soon arrested and the money was recovered.

On May 20, 1920, a jury pondered the case for 90 minutes before returning a guilty verdict. Hali spent four years in jail, but later found a job as a guard at Iolani Palace. And thus ended Hawaii's one and only Great Train Robbery.

Which community boomed following the Chinatown fire of 1900?

WHEN DEVELOPERS THEODORE LANSING and A.V. Gear created Hawaii's first subdivision in 1897, the response was less than enthusiastic. Their 520 acres of land along Waialae Avenue in Kaimuki were offered in 5-acre lots for $400-500 (about $8-10,000 today).

Many felt it was "too far from town." Back then Waialae was only a dirt road, as most streets were. Wild ostriches roamed the area, having been turned loose in 1896 by Dr. Trousseau, King Kalakaua's court physician.

The Great Chinatown fire of 1900 caused many to move to the new subdivision of Kaimuki. Honolulu Advertiser *photo.*

Then, something happened. A small fire was started in Chinatown in 1900 to battle the bubonic plague and it got out of hand. Before it could be stopped, most of Chinatown was in ruins.

Hundreds were homeless, and many turned to Kaimuki for housing.

Developers lowered their prices and offered an incentive — $50 for every baby born there.

The Pottery was once one of the nicest restaurants in Kaimuki. Hawaii State Archive photo.

A small zoo was built at 12th and Waialae Avenues, near the end of the trolley line, to entice visitors. The streetcar line was extended from Kapahulu Avenue in 1903. Many of the streets were paved and sidewalks laid by 1925.

It worked. Kaimuki caught on, and by 1939, the *Honolulu Advertiser* called it "the Territory of Hawaii's greatest single residential district."

By then, Kaimuki marked the end of Honolulu. Beyond that, to east Oahu, lay farms and dairies. The farms were relatively dark at night and Kaimuki had bright lights. Farmers referred to it as the "Big City," and Lane and Murphy Muraoka named their diner after it.

Kaimuki was a place for many firsts. Hawaii's first 7-Eleven (named for its original hours of operation), was on Waialae Ave. ABC Stores began in Kaimuki. And Kaimuki was the first place on Oahu to start night shopping, on Wednesday nights.

The H-1 Freeway began in Kaimuki. The entrance to the Mauka Arterial, as it was first called, was the Waialae entrance, just above U.H. The first section went as far as Bingham Street in 1953.

Kaimuki is commonly pronounced Kai-mu-ki, which is incorrect. The name is actually Ka-imu-ki. Ka means "the." Imu is an "oven for cooking" and ki refers to "ti root."

Some interesting facts about Kaimuki

The Kaimuki Zoo

Oahu's first zoological garden was the Kaimuki Zoo, erected at Waialae and Koko Head Avenues in 1905. Offering such attractions as animals, fish, birds, a Japanese tea house, Hawaiian grass houses, vaudeville, dancing, a roller skating rink, tennis courts, croquet grounds, bowling alley, and theater, it survived two years.

Not all the animals at the Kaimuki Zoo were authentic. A rainstorm washed away the stripes on the zebra to reveal it was really a donkey.

The view from Puu O Kaimuki Park, looking Mauka over the fire station. Honolulu Advertiser *photo.*

When the Kaimuki Zoo closed around 1907, the Outrigger Canoe Club bought its two grass houses and transported them to Waikiki on a borrowed truck. They became its first clubhouse.

Queen Lydia Liliuokalani Elementary School was built on the former zoo site. The oldest school in Kaimuki, was personally dedicated by the Queen on April 12, 1912.

Leahi Hospital

What we know today as Leahi Hospital began in 1900 in Chinatown as the "Honolulu Home for the Incurables." It treated tuberculosis and Hansen's disease patients. It moved to Kaimuki in 1902 and was renamed Leahi Home in 1906.

Fort Ruger

Fort Ruger was originally established in 1906 as a seacoast artillery post, known as the Diamond Head Military Reservation. Oahu was once ringed with defensive artillery batteries and Ruger was one of them.

When Oahu was finally attacked in 1945, the Japanese aircraft carriers were over 100 miles away and the artillery batteries were useless. Kapiolani Community College now uses much of the fort's acreage.

The fort was named for Brig. General Thomas Howard Ruger, who served the Union Army during the American Civil War and later was superintendent of West Point.

The most well loved facility on the base was Fort Ruger's Officers Club, called the Cannon Club. It opened on the slopes of Diamond Head in 1945 and overlooked Waikiki. The army closed it in 1997 after 52 years of operation.

Diamond Head Theatre

Thousands of us have attended plays at the Diamond Head Theatre over the years. Did you know it's the third oldest, continuously operating theatre in the entire United States?

Its roots can actually be traced to 1915, when a theatrical group called The Footlights was formed. Their first performance was *The Amazons* at the Honolulu Opera House, where the downtown Post Office on Merchant Street now stands.

During World War II, Honolulu Community Theatre productions entertained thousands of troops at over 300 performances throughout the Pacific.

In 1952, the Honolulu Community Theatre took over the Fort Ruger Theatre, the Army Post's former movie house. Then, in 1990, the name was changed to Diamond Head Theatre. Each season they offer six theatrical productions, including five major musicals, on a scale that rivals Broadway.

Waialae Country Club

The first development in what is now Kahala was Paul Isenberg's Waialae Ranch in 1884. The Royal Hawaiian Hotel built a golf course on the site in 1927. Local golfers could pay an annual fee

Waialae Country Club in the 1930s. Hawaii State Archives photo.

to join the Waialae Golf Club. Several of them created the Waialae Country Club in 1930.

Several holes on the golf course are modeled after famous golf courses around the world: The 10th Hole has features of the Road Hole at St. Andrews in Scotland. The 16th hole is similar to the sixth hole of the National Course at Southhampton, Long Island. The 13th is designed to resemble one on the Biarritz Course in France.

The first Hawaiian Open was held at Waialae in 1928. It became part of the PGA Tour in 1965.

Kahala Hilton

Local developer Charles Pietsch teamed up with Conrad Hilton to build the Kahala Hilton. The vision was of a hotel as fine as the Royal Hawaiian, but outside of Waikiki.

For months, they argued over what to name the hotel. Pietsch wanted Kahala Hilton. Conrad Hilton wanted to call it the Waialae Hilton. Finally Pietsch challenged Hilton to spell Waialae. Hilton stumbled, and realized a difficult to spell name would not be a good choice for the hotel.

The Kahala is famous for its dolfins. They arrived unintentionally. Nearby Sea Life Park needed a place to hold two of its dolfins while tanks were repaired, and Kahala Hitlon said yes. They proved such a big hit with guests, that after they were returned, the hotel brought in its own dolfins.

Waialae High School?

Kalani High was originally to be called Waialae High School when it opened in 1958. Its name was changed to honor Prince Jonah Kuhio Kalanianaole, who served in the U.S. Congress from 1903 until 1922. It was he who authored the Hawaiian Homes Commission Act in 1921.

KDI

THE WAILANA COFFEE HOUSE is open 24 hours a day, but do you recall what preceded it on the property? Before 1969, it was the Kapiolani Drive Inn, or more affectionately called KDI by its fans.

KDI was one of several Hawaii drive-ins that rode a wave of popularity in the 1950s and 1960s. Mary and Francis Tom built it on the corner of Ala Moana and Ena Road in 1949, when it was considered to be the outskirts of Waikiki. Mary even remembers counting cars that went by one evening — three. She says it scared her, but eventually the community found them.

KDI could hold over 100 cars, but a line often snaked out onto the street on weekend nights, after proms, or when they held their famous 5 hamburgers for $1 specials. Fourteen car hops would take your order and serve you.

Even more famous was their moving neon hula girl and ukulele guy sign atop the building.

Kapiolani Drive Inn began around 1947 at Kapiolani Park, when the zoo was called Waikiki Bird Park. They moved to Ena Road when a fence was put up at the park around 1949.

In 1969, the Toms saw that drive-ins were diminishing in popularity and transformed KDI into Wailana Coffee House and the 24-story condominium above it.

Left: Kapiolani Drive Inn moved from Kapiolani Park to the corner of Ala Moana and Ena Road in 1949. Mary and Francis Tom turned it into the Wailana Coffee House in 1969. Below: Looking over KDI, you can see the Hilton Hawaiian Village Dome, designed by Buckminster Fuller in 1957. Honolulu Advertiser photos. Right: A menu from the late 1940s when the Zoo was called Waikiki Bird Park.

Which event was created because tourists had trouble taking pictures of hula dancers at nightly luaus?

TOURISTS IN THE MID 1930s had a problem. They went to luaus at night and took pictures of the singers and dancers, but the low light and poor cameras caused the pictures to come out too dark to see.

Which event was created to solve this problem? Answer: The Kodak Hula Show.

Fritz Herman, then-vice president and manager of Kodak Hawaii saw the poor pictures daily. Ten years after the Royal Hawaiian Hotel opened in Waikiki, and in the midst of the Great Depression, he and Louise Akeo Silva started a daytime hula show at San Souci. Fritz's purpose was to sell film.

The Kodak Hula Show began in 1937 near San Soucci Beach. Honolulu Advertiser *photos.*

The free show started off slowly in 1937, long before the Kaimana Beach Hotel was built. The Natatorium was there, as was a grass shack. Herman found a spot on the grass where his hula girls, poi pounders and tree climbers could work.

There would always be at least a dozen dancers. Muumuu clad ukulele ladies played and sang. And, of course, there was the "hula lesson," where tourists were brought up to learn the dance and provide comic relief.

The show grew from once a week in the summer to four times a week year-round. Attendance grew to thousands a day. In the 62 years Kodak sponsored the show, it's estimated that 20 million attended. They may have taken over 100 million photos.

During World War II when tourism plummeted, the show performed for military audiences at USO shows.

At one point, there were bleachers that could hold hundreds on the grass behind the beach at San Souci. Soon after Frank Fasi became Mayor, in 1969, he ordered them removed from City

Up to 4,000 visitors attended Kodak Hula Show performances.

property. He also wanted to demolish the Natatorium. Governor Burns rescued the show, allowing it to move to Kapiolani Park near the Waikiki Shell.

Burns rescued another great project when Fasi decided the city would not build Aloha Stadium, but that's another story. The Kodak Arena was given a new set, with tikis, a canoe, coconut trees, landscaping, thatched roof huts, and bleachers that could hold 4,000.

The show was a Hawaii institution, but times change. Cameras and film improved. Countless photo opportunities were offered to tourists. Attendance probably reached its peak in the 1970s. By the 1990s, it dropped to about 2,000, and in the end, was less than 1,000 a day.

Kodak pulled out after 62 years and the Hogan Family Foundation took over for three more years. When it closed in 1992, it was the longest-running show in the world.

Auntie May Brown joined the show in 1938 as a 12-year-old, and took over when Aunty Louise Silva died in 1980. "When I first heard the show was ending, I was kind of happy," Brown told *Honolulu* magazine. "I mean, 65 years. Enough is enough."

"But, at the same time, it was really was heartbreaking for me to hear the show would end after all these years," Brown concedes. "It was one of the greatest experiences of my life."

Star-Bulletin editor Urban Allen called the Kodak Hula Show "one of the most potent means of advertising Hawaii to potential visitors. Its fame has spread around the world in countless amateur slide shows and movie performances that have contributed to kindling the spark of desire that brought subsequent visitors to the islands."

Which Oahu community was named for an 1840 downtown house?

John Papa Iʻi was a close advisor of Kamehameha III and foster father of Princess Victoria Kamamalu.

THE HOUSE belonged to John Iʻi. His great-great-grandson, DeSoto Brown says he raised Princess Victoria Kamamalu. "She was his hanai daughter," Brown says, "and he named his house *Mililani* for her."

The home was across from Iolani Palace, near King St. and makai of where the Judiciary Building stands today. It's called Mililani Street, today.

"Mili" means to caress. "Lani" is heavenly, and refers to Kamamalu's royal status. Another definition is "beloved place of chiefs."

John Iʻi was born in 1810 and was an attendant to Kamehameha III. Princess Victoria Kamamalu was born in 1838 and was a granddaughter of King Kamehameha I and sister

Princess Victoria Kamamalu was raised in the home called Mililani in her honor. Bishop Museum photos.

of Kamehameha IV and Kamehameha V.

As an adult, Kamamalu was once engaged to Prince William Lunalilo, but the wedding was called off. David Kalakaua was rumored to have also proposed to her, which she declined.

From 1854 to 1863, during the reign of Kamehameha IV, she was Kuhina Nui (prime minister) of the Kingdom. Kamamalu died on May 26, 1866, at the age of 27. She was the last female directly descended from Kamehameha the Great. She is sometimes confused with an older Victoria Kamamalu, who married Kamehameha II.

DeSoto Brown is now chief archivist at the Bishop Museum. He says Castle & Cooke was unaware that the name originally came from his great-great-grandfather's house, when they built the Central Oahu town of Mililani.

Many also think that Mililani was Hawaii's first planned community, but that distinction goes to Pearl City, built by Dillingham in 1890.

The name "Mililani" came from this home downtown in the 1850s.

Sonny Chillingworth and Makana

A T THE AGE OF 12, MAKANA WAS FEATURED playing slack key guitar on a TV program called *Superkids of summer.* "During a slack key guitar festival the following year, I had the wonderful opportunity of meeting Uncle Sonny backstage after his performance," Makana recalls. "Amazingly he had seen the TV show and was aware of my interest and potential as a student. Soon after, I was blessed to become his student, and we would often sit in his garage and jam together. Those were the days!"

Edwin Bradfield "Sonny" Chillingworth is a legend in the realm of Hawaiian music, especially the traditional art form of Hawaiian Slack Key Guitar. He began playing guitar at the age of 12, and after high school, found himself playing luaus and clubs with Andy Cummings and Gabby Pahinui.

"When I met Uncle Sonny, I was 13, and was at the time a 2-year protege of Robert Moderow Jr.," Makana says, "who had studied slack key under the Nanakuli Master Uncle Raymond Kane."

Sonny Chillingworth mentored a very young Makana. Honolulu Advertiser *photo.*

"Sonny was like a loving grandfather to me. He took me as his last student and taught me the necessary rudiments of his own approach to the art form, with heavy emphasis on proper technique (as Bobby had done so with Raymond's style) so as to instill deep roots from which I would be able to expand in the future. Beyond the technical training, he shared with me something much more valuable: an intimate and heartfelt love for this uniquely Hawaiian expression of music, known to Kanaka Maoli as 'Ki Ho'alu.'"

Sonny Chillingworth was one of the most influential Hawaiian slack key guitar masters in history. "His style showcased a high technical proficiency that inspires generations of players to this day, and his voice is at once recognizable, with its operatic quality being so unique to the genre. His soulfulness, and his dedication to the perpetuation as well as the evolution of slack key through teaching, recording and performing is a great gift to all who appreciate this beautiful music."

"To this day, anytime I am on-stage in a performance, I feel Sonny's presence," Makana says, "as well as other Kupuna, guiding me and even contributing to the great sound that comes forth from my kika ki ho'alu (slack key guitar)."

Makana spent two months on the mainland in 2007, and his performances were all well received and attended. Visit www.myspace.com/makanaworld to stay current on him.

"The fans have been really supportive and open to all of the new directions in my music. I've been continuing my style expansion, which at present includes Hawaiian slack key, traditional and contemporary Hawaiian music, other cultural music (like Portuguese and Bossa Nova), folk, rock, blues and jazz, and ambient music. My passion is music as exploration. What allows me to keep expanding is the foundation (roots) given me as a young man by the Kupuna."

The first time Marilyn Monroe felt like a star

A YEAR AFTER THE RELEASE OF "GENTLEMEN Prefer Blondes," 28-year-old Marilyn Monroe married Joe DiMaggio. They stopped in Hawaii on the way to their honeymoon in Japan at the Kawana Hotel. A crowd of over 1,000 people greeted the blonde and the baseball hero at Honolulu Airport on Saturday, January 30, 1954.

Local Sgt. James Cullen shook hands with DiMaggio and put a lei around Marilyn's neck and kissed her on the cheek. A team of police ringed the couple and escorted them through the crowd to their powder blue convertible and to the Royal Hawaiian Hotel.

The next day they flew to Japan. Associated Press reporter Jim

Joe DiMaggio and Marilyn Monroe were greeted by 1,000 people at Honolulu Airport on their Honeymoon in 1954. Honolulu Advertiser photo.

Becker, who'd later write for the *Star-Bulletin* was staying at the Kawana Hotel in Shizuoka, and interviewed them. The Army read about them and asked Marilyn to come to Korea to entertain the troops. Even though the Korean War was over, 400,000 troops remained.

Marilyn's response to the colonel who came to ask her was, "Good God, No," Becker reported "I have never been on a stage in my life. I have no act. I know the words to only two songs and have nothing to wear!" Silence.

Joe encouraged her to go anyway and support the troops. Joe stayed in Japan while his new wife went with a friend and Jim Becker to Korea. He described her as "fresh as paint, eager to embrace life, so keen to please, and so vulnerable."

She performed 10 times in the dead of winter, with temperatures sometimes below zero, in her one purple sequined dress. She sang the same two songs, *Diamonds are a girl's best friend*, and *Two little girls from Little Rock*, but it didn't matter. She received standing ovations. Becker describes the reception as "enthusiastic to the point of hysteria."

Back in Japan, Marilyn told Joe, "you never heard such cheering," but Joe replied, "oh, yes I have."

The press in Honolulu asked her, on her return, about the trip. She said the Japanese people were charming, but the Japanese press asked rather personal questions — like whether she wore panties, slept without nightclothes, or how she got her famous walk.

"American newsmen asked me the same questions. The Japanese press simply was more direct about it."

"The reception of the troops was fantastic," the actress said. "When I got on stage they cheered for a full five minutes before I could say anything. It was a beautiful sound. It was the first time I really felt like a star." —*Researched by Brandi Boatner*

Before Victoria Ward Center

Car lots, warehouses, and a few retailers occupied what is now Victoria Ward Center in 1970. Looking Ewa, Auahi Street is on the right, and Ala Moana is on the left. Honolulu Advertiser photo.

CURTIS PERRY WARD AND HIS WIFE VICTORIA bought 12 acres of land for $2,450 in 1870 and soon added another 90 acres. Curtis was from Kentucky and wanted an estate that reminded him of home. They built an estate they called "Old Plantation" in 1882.

Surrounded by hundreds of trees, the site hosted a beautiful home and a large lagoon, on what was then considered to be the outskirts of Honolulu.

Curtis died later that year. Victoria carried on with her seven daughters. When the last one passed away around 1950, it opened the question of what to do with the estate, which, at one time extended from Thomas Square to Kewalo Basin.

The city considered using the King Street property as a police station or war memorial auditorium. The old Honolulu Civic Auditorium at 1314 South King Street was too small and old and the city needed a bigger, newer facility.

HPD ended up moving into the old Sears building at Beretania and Kalakaua. The Ward Estate was purchased in 1958 for $2 million and the Honolulu International Center opened in 1964. It was renamed Neal S. Blaisdell Center in 1975 in honor of the former Honolulu mayor.

The Victoria Ward Ltd. staff wrestled in the late 1960s about what to do with the 65 acres they owned along Ala Moana Blvd. At the time, there were warehouses, light industries, a few car dealers and retail stores.

They're names are famous, but not their faces. Curtis Perry Ward, left; Victoria Ward, right.
Hawaii State Archives photos.

Their first idea, named the West Kewalo Plan, called for hotels to be built and twin condominium towers that would house 6,000 people. The community resisted the plan, fearing Ala Moana beach would be overrun by tourists.

Instead, the estate turned to retailing and light industrial uses. Ward Warehouse was built in 1975 and Ward Center in 1982. Victoria Ward Centers today has 140 shops and restaurants. Ala Moana Center owner, General Growth Properties of Chicago, bought Victoria Ward Center in 2002 for $250 million.

The Honolulu Civic Auditorium at 1314 So. King St. was opened in 1933 and torn down in 1974. It was the largest facility for concerts, conventions, basketball, boxing, roller derbies and wrestling. Honolulu Advertiser photo.

Where did the name 'Hawaii Calls' come from?

N O, IT'S NOT A phone call. A "call" is a shortwave radio term for the transmission that preceded a broadcast. The "call" reassured the network that the show was about to begin, and that it was actually going to "come through."

Well over 400 radio stations on the mainland, 50 in Canada,

Webley Edwards created "Hawaii Calls." It broadcast for 40 years and caused millions to visit our shores. Honolulu Advertiser *photo.*

175 in Europe, Australia and Japan, and 130 military stations carried *Hawaii Calls* each week to millions of listeners. It created a wave of interest in Hawaiian music and planted a seed about visiting our shores.

Webley Edwards created *Hawaii Calls* in 1935. He was visiting a San Francisco radio station that played some "un-Hawaiian Hawaiian music." Edwards said that the music was being played by people who had never been to Hawaii.

The studio executives said, "why don't you get us some of the real stuff?" Edwards' answer to the challenge was to begin *Hawaii Calls* on July 5, 1935.

Edwards teamed up with Al Kealoha Perry (whose wife opened the Willows in 1944) as his musical director. CBS gave him a two-week trial run. The show ran for an astonishing 40 years.

They broadcast from "beneath the banyan tree" at the Moana

Hotel, and used real waves crashing on the shore in the broadcast.

"The people of Hawaii bid you welcome," Edwards would say with the sounds of the sea in the background. "Hawaii Calls."

To listeners on the mainland during the Great Depression, in the years before television, the broadcast must have seemed like a connection to paradise. Over 1,000 tourists attended most broadcasts. Why was the show so successful, Edwards was asked? "For one reason or another, people all over the world want Hawaiian music played by Hawaiians from Hawaii," was his reply.

Edwards would regularly give the air and water temperature at Waikiki Beach, but stopped it in the belief that he was irritating snow-bound listeners. Their response was a barrage of complaints and the feature was quickly put back into the half-hour show.

Webley Edwards came to Hawaii in 1928 to play semi-pro football. He had been the quarterback at Oregon State and the Town Team hired him. He also sold cars for Schuman Carriage.

Besides its powerful lure for tourists, *Hawaii Calls* also made many Hawaiian singers and their songs world famous. *Sweet*

Al Kealoha Perry was Hawaii Calls' musical director.

Leilani, Beyond the Reef, Lovely Hula Hands, Quiet Village, and the Hawaiian Wedding Song are just a few of the songs that *Hawaii Calls* brought to a wide audience.

Edwards hosted *Hawaii Calls* until 1972, when he suffered a stroke. The show went off the air in 1975 and Edwards died a year later. His ashes were scattered in the waters off Waikiki, near the Moana Hotel and its famous banyan tree.

Which King's Summer Palace lies in ruins in Nuuanu?

HIDDEN DEEP IN THE FORESTS OF NUUANU, and old structure suddenly appears on a hiking trail. It looks like the ruins of a small house. A marker in front tells an even more improbable tale — more than 10,000 people attended a luau here in 1847.

The cottage was built for Kamehameha III and his wife, Queen Kalama in 1845. The 900 square foot home is referred to as their summer palace. Its name, Kaniakapupu, means the sound of the land snails.

Historians point out that Nuuanu back then was more open and grassy. Sugar growers brought in ironwood and pines to cool the island and cause more rainfall in the 1920s. The Civilian Conservation Corps planted bamboo and eucalyptus in the 1930s.

Former *Honolulu Advertiser* columnist Bob Krauss pointed out that Kaniakapupu was in use more than a decade before the Queen Emma Summer Palace was built, and 40 years before King Kalakaua built Iolani Palace.

A historic marker was put up in the last 30 years and it describes "the scene of entertainment of foreign celebrities and the feasting of chiefs and commoners" on July 31, 1847 — Restoration Day.

All that remains of King Kamehameha III's Summer Palace in Nuuanu are these ruins and a marker. Honolulu Advertiser photos.

King Kamehameha III arrived in a carriage drawn by four horses. The carriage had been a gift from England's Queen Victoria to Tahiti's Queen Pomare. Three hundred uniformed troops escorted the King to Beretania Street, but remained to stand guard in the now-deserted town. "Young chiefs on horseback followed the carriage," Krauss said. "Then came 1,000 women on horseback, riding five abreast and gaily dressed. The Punchbowl battery fired a 21-gun salute as the King crossed Beretania Street into what was then considered to be "the country."

A man hired to count horses crossing a bridge reported 4,600 — the heaviest traffic the bridge had seen.

The menu included 55 ducks, 71 hogs, 1,820 fresh fish, 3,125 salt fish, three oxen, 602 chickens, four barrels of onions, 12 barrels of luau and cabbage, 10 barrels of potatoes, 2,245 coconuts, 482 large calabashes of poi, 1,000 heads of taro, and 180 squid. It was the largest luau in Hawaii history.

Kauikeaouli became King Kamehameha III at age 11. Print by Rob Dampier.

Hardly a trace of Kaniakapupu remains today. The forest has overgrown the small building, and few are even aware that it's there.

Kamehameha III's Summer Palace as it may have looked in 1850. Drawing by Paul Emmert. .

What locations were considered for the State Capitol?

T HE DEBATE BEGAN IN 1949 AND TOOK TEN years to conclude. The issue was, where to build a needed state capitol? Hundreds of lawyers, architects, elected officials and citizens suggested and debated over 20 potential capitol locations. They were:

Aala Park
Ala Wai Golf Course
Civic Center
Diamond Head
Fort Armstrong
Fort DeRussy
Honolulu Rapid Transit Block
Iolani Palace
Magic Island
Maui and Kauai

Oahu Country Club
Pali Golf Course area
Punchbowl
Sand Island
Thomas Square
Upper Bishop Street
Waianae-kai
Ward Estate
Washington Place

The Civic Center site, where the capitol was finally built, was once occupied by several buildings, including the state armory along Beretania, and the Schumann Carriage auto dealership, at Richards Street. A Shell service station could be found at Punchbowl and Hotel, and Iolani Barracks was next to it. Miller Street, which now leads to the underground parking, formerly crossed Beretania and ended at Hotel Street.

At eight acres, the Civic Center was centrally located but was felt by the Citizens Committee and Planning Director to be "too small, congested, not expandable, lacks prominence and setting. It can never be anything but the backyard to Iolani Palace," they said.

The seashore location at the Fort Armstrong entrance to Honolulu Harbor was thought to be a beautiful location for a state capitol. Supporters, led by Frank Fasi, suggested much of it would be built on reclaimed reef. Detractors said it would be in danger of a tsunami, and was surrounded by industry, making it impractical.

"Harold Castle offered to donate 100 acres of land across from the Pali Golf Course in Windward Oahu, where Hawaii Pacific University is today," says Kaneohe Ranch President Mitch D'Olier

This is what the State Capitol grounds looked like in 1960. Iolani Palace looks the same, but everything else is different. Hotel Street runs through the center of the photo. Miller Street can be seen crossing Beretania Street at the bottom before ending at Hotel Street. The larger building on Miller and Hotel Streets was the State Armory. Iolani Barracks was to its left. Honolulu Advertiser photo.

The setting was beautiful and the size was ample for any conceivable future demand, supporters argued. And, of course, the price was right. But it was a 20-minute drive from Honolulu.

Architect Alfred Preis, who designed the Arizona Memorial, urged the state to build the capitol at Aala Park, and land makai to Nimitz Highway. Its chief virtue was that it was twice the size of the Civic Center space.

Louise Dillingham and 50 women's clubs suggested staying at Iolani Palace. Wings could be added to Iolani Palace on both sides for the House and Senate. More buildings could be added to the palace grounds, they felt.

In 1957, Governor Oren Long proposed building the capitol and

Iolani Barracks was moved and rebuilt about 100 yards away on Richards Street. Hawaii State Archives photo.

an auditorium to replace the Civic Auditorium on the 146-acre Ala Wai Golf Course. Golfers know the Ala Wai is always proposed as the site for any large endeavor. They flexed their political muscle and politicians found another location.

Vincent Esposito led some state legislators in suggesting Sand Island. Many states have capitols away from large urban areas, Maui and Kauai pointed out. Why not another island?

Finally, exhausted legislators in 1959 selected the current, Civic Center site. They believed that the legislature and governor must be near state government departments and City and Federal offices. In May of 1959, Governor Quinn signed a bill designating the downtown Civic Center site.

Imagine, however, if it was at the entrance to Honolulu Harbor, at Aala Park, or in Windward Oahu … .

The now gone corner of Hotel and Punchbowl Streets in 1964 hosted a Shell service station. Next to it was Iolani Barracks and the State Armory. Hawaii State Archives photo.

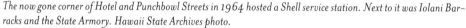

Who is called the Ambassador of Aloha?

Danny Kaleikini is Hawaii's "Ambassador of Aloha."

NEED A HINT? He's from Papakolea, one of 12 children. He's a mix of Irish, Korean, Chinese, and Hawaiian. He had what was probably the longest running nightclub show in America — 28 years.

He can welcome audiences in Chinese, Japanese, Korean, Tagalog, French, Italian, Greek, Arabic. "Everywhere I go, aloha is stamped on my forehead," Danny says. "I'm spreading the word."

"I was brought up with Aloha in the family — it was all we had! Aloha is something you cannot buy," Kaleikini continues. "It's a communicable disease; you lose it if you don't communicate it. Your aloha goes out to others. My friend Abraham Akaka says aloha is the breath of life you give to others."

"Hawaiian songs are a good way of getting it across. Hawaiian music is soothing and romantic. The songs tell us about the old Hawaii, the islands of long ago, and how people felt." Kaniela was the 1979 Aloha Week Ambassador of Aloha and in 1988, Gov. Waihee officially declared him Hawaii's Ambassador of Aloha.

Kaleikini, who used to sell newspapers and shine shoes near the Hawaii Theater, got the encouragement to pursue a singing career at weekend jam sessions at a Charley's Taxi stand downtown, where the Kamamalu Building now stands.

Cab drivers would gather on Friday and Saturday nights in the 1940s and 1950s, to play music at their stand on King and Richards Streets. Kaleikini began attending those jam sessions and his great voice and personal charm was noticed and appreciated by the others.

"Danny received a lot of applause and tips, but also encouragement to pursue a professional career," says Dale Evans, owner and daughter of Charley's Taxi. "Eddie Kamae and the Kalima Brothers also got their start at these jam sessions."

Danny grew up idolizing Hawaiian entertainers like Ray Kinney and Alfred Apaka. One of his first real jobs was at Aunty Becky's Place in Kihei, Maui, where he got $10 a night, plus a room and kau kau. Danny sang, wiped tables, washed dishes and raked the yard.

Kaleikini was one of Roosevelt High School's top singers. Honolulu Advertiser *photos.*

Sterling Mossman occasionally invited Danny to perform at the Barefoot Bar. Ray Kinney took him to the Royal Hawaiian Hotel and taught him stage mannerisms: "How to smile, how to talk, and I learned all over again how to sing and project. I couldn't have learned in college what I learned on that Monarch Room Stage."

Danny became the emcee for Hilo Hattie's show. However, one Christmas he found himself on stage dressed as a mynah bird "in one papaya tree." He learned one thing — "never be a mynah bird again!"

He got some jobs in Canada, Puerto Rico, and Havana, Cuba. "Fidel Castro came to the show one night. In the Caribbean, I worked with a Hawaiian group, but only three of us were real Hawaiians. The others were Mexican! The Mexicans danced hula and no one knew they weren't Hawaiian until they spoke."

"I used to play drums, I used to play the ukulele. I sang. One year I even danced knife. I thought I was going to kill everybody. 'Oh, can you throw my knife back, please. It wasn't supposed to go that way.'"

His show at the Kahala Hilton began on April 26, 1967 a year after the hotel opened. It was far from Waikiki, and the hotel was only averaging 25% occupancy. Danny had no contract. "It was pure guts," he said in 1987. "Whatever business we generated, that's what we got."

Danny's show was very interactive. He'd talk to individuals in the crowd, find out where they were from and then sing them a song in their native language. Within two years, he caught on, and put on over 12,000 performances in 28 years.

Kaleikini says he wasn't the star of the show at the Kahala Hilton Hala Terrace. "We were all family, ohana at the show. I'm just the kumu. "There's only room for one star. And that's God upstairs. Plus, you know, God is Hawaiian!" Danny then pretended to be God: "Hey, you guys, listen up! Alooooooooooooha!"

"On one occasion, I walked off the stage and gave a lei to a lady," Danny recalled. "When I walked away, her wig was stuck on my sleeve button! I put it back on her head and it was crooked. The husband laughed. Everybody started laughing. I was so embarrassed. I kept apologizing. I kept laughing too."

The man from the "Hawaiian Beverly Hills of Papakolea" retired from the Kahala Hilton in 1995 after 28 years. He's spent time with many boards, charities, golf and family.

"I thank God he gave me a talent," he says. "Because of this talent, I got to see the world. I've sung for kings, queens, and presidents. I've sung for dignitaries, I've sung for real people, regular people. All of it because of aloha."

Kaleikini performed for 28 years at the Kahala Hilton. Aloooooooooha.

Remembering John Bellinger

JOHN BELLINGER WAS THE YOUNGEST PRESIDENT of First Hawaiian Bank when he took over at 45 in 1969. Nearly twenty years since his death in 1989, he is still fondly remembered for his leadership and friendship.

It was Bellinger who first crossed racial lines and lent money from a "haole bank" to a local company in 1962 — for Aloha Airlines to buy jets.

Goro Arakawa recalls Bellinger wanting to buy an entire bolt of yellow palaka material to have shirts made. "I had to take him to the factory that made our shirts," Arakawa recalls. "It looked great on him. A few months later, at his funeral, many of his staff were wearing yellow palaka."

Brig. General Fred Weyand, retired Army Chief of Staff, and now on First Hawaiian's Board of Directors says "there was something about John Bellinger. He had a fatherly aura about him. People just looked up to him as an authority. That's why he was very successful as CEO."

After Weyand joined the bank in 1976, "John Bellinger took me aside, and said, there's only one thing I want you to remember: there's only one general in this bank and that's me."

"Bellinger was able to bond with senior officials and businessmen in Japan. He exuded honesty and integrity. I went with him to call on big accounts in Japan, and he called on the richest man in Japan at the time, Yoshiaki Tsutsumi."

"Johnny went up to the 23rd floor to meet with him. When they were through with their meeting, he escorted Johnny to the elevator, got in the elevator with him, took him downstairs, and escorted him to his automobile."

"It was apparently something a Japanese official never did," Weyand believes. "It became quite a story in Japan that the richest man would honor Bellinger in that manner."

His successor at the bank, Walter Dods called Bellinger "a leader with a big heart." Bellinger had been a star football player at Roosevelt High School. "He was the only wide receiver that I know of, in the history of Hawaii football, who called all the plays." Usually it's the quarterback or coach. Dods says it was a sign of the businessman he would become.

Fred Weyand, left, says John Bellinger had a fatherly aura about him. People just looked up to him as an authority. Honolulu Advertiser *photo.*

Which on-line news media was inadvertently created by Gov. Cayetano?

H AWAII JOURNALISTS MALIA ZIMMERMAN and Jay McWilliams, formerly of *Pacific Business News*, launched HawaiiReporter.com in 2002. The daily on-line news journal covers local and national education, business, government and political stories. They attract more than 1 million visitors a month.

The main reason *Hawaii Reporter* exists is because of the inadvertent actions of former Gov. Benjamin Cayetano.

Jay McWilliams, Malia Zimmerman and Laura Brown celebrated Hawaii Reporter's 5th anniversary in 2007.

Zimmerman, a front-page investigative reporter for *Pacific Business News* since 1997, wrote about government scandals, corruption and unfair treatment of businesses. Cayetano took the stories personally and made it his mission to target her and *PBN*.

One series accused Cayetano of using state agencies, such as the attorney general, the tax department, and the Department of Labor's HIOSH division, to investigate, punish and ultimately close down the businesses of his enemies.

Cayetano threatened to cut off *PBN's* access to his administrators and himself. Reports were coming in that he was starting to lean on advertisers to pull their ads. *The Wall Street Journal* wrote a scathing attack on Cayetano for his retaliation against Zimmerman but, nonetheless, *PBN* fired her.

He might have thought he had won, but instead, she and McWilliams founded *Hawaii Reporter*. As the traditional media has cut staff and limited investigative reporting, *Hawaii Reporter* has stepped into the opportunity.

Hawaii Reporter investigations led *ABC 20/20* to report on the Ka Loko Dam breach. While much of the media reports on the development of rail transit, *Hawaii Reporter* has been almost alone in pointing out problems other U.S. cities have had. No mass transit rail system has ever reduced traffic congestion in any U.S. city.

Hawaii Reporter was the first to report on the legal case that Duke Bainum's wife, Jennifer Toma, was involved in, with the family of Masumi Murasaki. The family had accused Toma of wrongly taking nearly $1 million from the 83-year-old man she cared for.

Hawaii Reporter also broke the story about an American Savings Bank assistant manager who took over $1 million from a customer. Zimmerman was the first to uncover problems with Sen. Cal

Kawamoto's campaign fund, which led to his ousting by voters in the 2004 election.

Hawaii Reporter won the top investigative reporting award from the Society of Professional Journalists in 2002 for exposing the horrendous treatment of Vietnamese workers in a garment factory in American Samoa.

The *Wall Street Journal, Washington Times, UPI, Fox News, National Review,* the *Associated Press* and other publications across the world have published or quoted *Hawaii Reporter*.

KSSK's Michael W. Perry said he uses "*Hawaii Reporter* to give the seldom-heard 'other side of the story' in our local media. Malia and the gang are must-reads for me everyday."

Gov. Cayetano's interference ultimately pushed the women into a whole new direction and gave them the "freedom to report the real news" (now their company slogan) they never enjoyed in the traditional mainstream media.

Who dat 1 ???

Here are nine Hawaii high school yearbook pictures of some well known politicians, newscasters, and celebrities.Can you place the face? Answers on page 234

1. Punahou 1979

2. Kahuku 1970

3. Radford 1963

4. Kamehameha 1949

5. Iolani 1972

6. Farrington 1958

7. Kamehameha 1969

8. Damien 1962

9. Kamehameha 1942

Who dat 2 ???

Here are nine Hawaii high school yearbook pictures of some well known politicians, newscasters, and celebrities. Can you place the face? Answers on page 234

10. Punahou 1980

11. Kamehameha 1966

12. Kamehameha 1967

13. Hawaii Prep 1970

14. Roosevelt 1955

15. Sacred Hearts 1984

16. Roosevelt 1954

17. Punahou 1967

18. McKinley 1962

Who dat 3 ???

Here are nine Hawaii high school yearbook pictures of some well known politicians, newscasters, and celebrities. Can you place the face? Answers on page 234

19. *Lahainaluna 1979*

20. *Roosevelt 1987*

21. *McKinley 1944*

22. *Radford 1961*

23. *Punahou 1954*

24. *Saint Louis, 1961*

25. *Castle 1980*

26. *Kalani 1972*

27. *Punahou 1972*

How well do you know Rap Reiplinger?

Answers on page 235

Rap Reiplinger was one of Hawaii's zaniest comedians. How well do you remember his humor? See if you can answer the question or complete the following lines from Rap's comedy routines.

1   Auntie Marialani: "Not too sweet, not too _____."

2   "Tell Fate Yanagi no go cry, and no go out with _____ ____"

3   Wendell's — home of the 12 inch _____ _____.

4   What was the name of the crisis hotline where Rap worked? _____ Hotline.

5   What problem did Barry, who called the hotline, have? _____

6   Mr. James Okada took a soda taste test. What did he like best? _____

7   Mr. Fogerty in room 1225 called Room Service and wanted to order what meal? _____, _____, and _____.

8   How did the room service operator pronounce his name? _____

9   Which actual Hawaii company was named for a Rap routine? _____ _____

10 Rap wrote a comedy skit that was a soap opera. What was the name of the skit? "Like sand in the BVDs, so are the lives of the _____ _____."

How well do you know Hawaii's Military?

Answers on page 235

Hawaii's relationship with the U.S. military goes back over 100 years. How well do you know Hawaii bases and military units?

1   A military reservation was built in this ancient Oahu volcanic crater in 1899 and housed several gun batteries. It became a cemetery in 1949. Name it.

2   For which war was Tripler built?

3   What was the name of the famous officer's club at Fort Ruger on the slopes of Diamond Head?

4   What nickname did the 442nd Army Division earn during World War II?

5   This military base was named for the beautiful objects sea creatures, that once inhabited the area, make when irritated.

6   Which base is called the "Pineapple Pentagon?"

7   The 25th Infantry Division's two-word nickname symbolized its speed, aggressive spirit, and South Pacific battles. What is its nickname?

8   Col. Billy Mitchell predicted in 1923 that the Japanese would attack Pearl Harbor. There were no aircraft carriers at that time. From what location would they have launched their attack?

9   What did Hawaii get in exchange for giving Pearl Harbor to the U.S. Military?

10 During World War II, the Navy used the Royal Hawaiian Hotel for R&R. The staff sealed up an important part of the hotel. After the war, they returned to learn that Navy personnel had never discovered it. What were they so interested in hiding?

How well do you know Hawaii Companies that were named for songs?

Answers on page 235

Many Hawaii companies have names that are associated with songs. Can you conjure up the company based on these clues?

1   This Ward Center restaurant's name comes from a song from the 1933 movie *Hollywood Party*. "You saw me standing alone, without a dream in my heart, without a love of my own."

2   Eva Narcissus Boyd sang a Carole King dance song that inspired the name of this surf shop.

3   The waiters were costumed at this Waikiki restaurant, which was named for a 1970 Janis Joplin song about freedom.

4   This Honolulu florist's name came from a 1937 song by Harry Owens, from the movie *Waikiki Wedding*.

5   A 1967 Rolling Stones song gave this Ala Moana restaurant its name. "She would never say where she came from."

6   The Korean national song has been applied to several bars and restaurants. The name means "beautiful dear."

7   One of Hawaii's largest stores for tourists is named for a 1935 dance song by McDiarmid & Noble. It catapulted the singer, a Royal Hawaiian Hotel Girl's Glee Club member, to national prominence.

8   Reid and Jonelle Fujita say their retail stores are not named for this 1969 Neil Young song.

9   A Mexican restaurant on Kapahulu is named for a 1958 Ritchie Valens' song.

10 A popular Kamuela restaurant shares the name of a song about a flower from the 1965 movie *The Sound of Music*. "Small and white, clean and bright, you look happy to meet me."

Hawaii Restaurant Quiz

Answers on page 235

You've eaten there since "small kid time." But can you guess which restaurant matches these clues?

1   Which Honolulu and Pearl City restaurants began as the Olympic Grill in 1950 on Ala Moana Blvd? Owner Steven Nagamine changed the name after a trip to Las Vegas.

2   This Hawaiian food restaurant on School Street in Kalihi is famous for its butterfish collars and pipikaula shortribs.

3   Which restaurant's name means "fish impression" in Japanese?

4   Hawaii's first banyan tree grows in the middle of this Honolulu restaurant, named for a carnivore with an appetite.

5   McDonald's founder Ray Kroc and several executives sampled saimin at a Kalihi restaurant before adding it to their menu. Which restaurant did they visit?

6   The founder of this Hawaiian food restaurant in Waipahu learned to cook at internment camps on the mainland during World Waw II.

7   This was Hawaii's first drive-in. It was famous for its Ono Ono shakes and Waffle Hot Dogs.

8   Spenceliff once owned 50 Hawaii restaurants. Only one remains. What is its name?

9   Bob Lee Sr. owned an Oahu dairy. It was named to honor him and his father. It became a soda fountain, and is now a chain of 200+ restaurants. What is its name?

10 The Hard Rock Café was the third restaurant to occupy the corner of Kalakaua and Kapiolani. Name a previous one.

Hawaii Sports Quiz

Answers on page 235

How well do you know some of Hawaii's top athletes?

1   This surfer was the "Queen of Makaha," and was Hawaii's first female lifeguard.

2   This Kauai native was the second Hawaii golfer, after Ted Makalena, to win a PGA tour event, when he captured the 1990 Hawaiian Open.

3   This man signed with the Los Angeles Rams as a free agent in 1967, and later was a U.H. football coach. Now he can be found on the radio dial.

4   This man dropped out of McKinley High School to swim at the 1912 Stockholm Olympics.

5   This school's basketball team scored one of the biggest upsets in sports history in 1982 with its 77-72 victory over the number-one ranked University of Virginia, led by 7'-4" Ralph Sampson.

6   This sports venue opened on Isenberg and King Streets in 1926 and was affectionately called "Termite Palace."

7   This sports legend played semi-pro football in Hawaii in 1941, and lived in Kaimuki, for six years before breaking the baseball color barrier as an L.A. Dodger.

8   This man was sumo's first yokozuna, or grand champion, born outside of Japan.

9   On August 26, 1939, the Baseball Hall of Fame opened. Baseball founder Alexander Joy Cartwright, who had lived in Hawaii, was honored. With what drink did players toast him before their game that day at Ebbets Field in Brooklyn?

Answers to Quizzes

Who Dat Answers

Who Dat 1
1. Barak Obama
2. Sam Choy
3. Bette Midler
4. Don Ho
5. Mufi Hannemann
6. Ben Cayetano
7. Keola Beamer
8. Frank De Lima
9. Dan Akaka

Who Dat 2
10. Kelly Preston
11. Kimo Kahoano
12. Robert Cazimero
13. Ed Case
14. Danny Kaleikini
15. Tia Carerra
16. Larry Price
17. Henry Kapono
18. Carole Kai

Who Dat 3
19. Kealii Reichel
20. Shawn Ching
21. George Ariyoshi
22. Melveen Leed
23. Al Harrington
24. Jim Leahey
25. Sharie Shima
26. Leslie Wilcox
27. Nainoa Thompson

Rap Reiplinger Quiz Answers:

1. Rancid; 2. Mits Funai; 3. Lau Lau; 4. Pilikia Hotline; 5. Ukus;
6. The crackers; 7. Cheeseburger, fries, and a thick chocolate malt;
8. Mr. Frog Tree; 9. Mahalo Airlines; 10 Young Kanakas.

Military Quiz Answers

1. The National Memorial Cemetery of the Pacific at Punchbowl;
2. Tripler began as the Fort Shafter Hospital in 1907, and was
built to handle casualties from the Spanish-American War;
3. The Cannon Club; 4. "Go for Broke;" 5.Pearl Harbor; 6. Fort
Shafter is the "Pineapple Pentagon;" 7. "Tropic Lightning;" 8. Niihau;
9. Duty free sugar exports; 10. The Royal Hawaiian Hotel hid its
expensive wine cellar, and the Navy never found it during WWII.

Companies named for Songs Answers

1. Brew Moon; 2. Local Motion (Locomotion); 3. Bobby McGee's;
4. Sweet Leilani; 5. Ruby Tuesday; 6. Arirang; 7. Hilo Hattie;
8. Cinnamon Girl; 9. La Bamba; 10. Edelweiss.

Hawaii Restaurant Quiz Answers

1. Flamingo; 2. Helena's Hawaiian Food; 3. Gyotaku; 4. Hungry
Lion; 5. Boulevard Saimin; 6. Highway Inn; 7. KC Drive-Inn;
8. Fisherman's Wharf; 9. L&L Hawaiian BBQ; 10. Coco's and
Kau Kau Korner.

Sports Quiz Answers

1. Rell Sunn; 2. David Ishii; 3. Larry Price; 4. Duke Kahanamoku;
5. Chaminade; 6. Honolulu Stadium; 7. Jackie Robinson;
8. Chad Rowen, Akebono; 9. Pineapple juice.

Bibliography

The following sources were used in the writing of this book.

Aloha Elvis — Jerry Hopkins.

Aloha Waikiki — 100 years of pictures from Hawaii's most famous beach, Desoto Brown.

Broken Trust — Samuel King and Randall Roth.

The Cheating of America - Charles Lewis and Bill Allison.

Firsts and Almost Firsts in Hawaii, Robert C. Schmitt.

Frank, Sammy, Marlon & Me — Eddie Sherman.

Hawaii Business magazine.

Hawaii Looking Back — an illustrated History of the islands, Glen Grant.

Hawaii's Forgotten History — Rich Budnick

Hawaii Sports: History, Facts & Statistics — Dan Cisco

The *Honolulu Advertiser.*

Honolulu Magazine.

The *Honolulu Star-Bulletin.*

Kahala — The Hotel that could only happen once, Ed Sheehan.

Malamalama — A history of the University of Hawaii, Robert Kamins and Robert Potter.

Oahu's Hidden History — William Dorrance.

Pocket Place Names in Hawaii, Mary Pukui, Samuel Elbert, Esther Mookini.

Saints, Sinners & Shortstops — Jim Becker.

Shipwrecked! — Rhoda Blumberg.

Stepping into time, A guide to Honolulu's Historic Landmarks, Jeannette Murray Peek.

Sweet Leilani: The Story Behind the Song — Harry Owens.

The Companies We Keep

If you enjoyed *The Companies We Keep 2*, you'll want to read the first book, *The Companies We Keep — Amazing stories about 450 of Hawaii's best known companies*.

Here are some of the fascinating stories you'll find in that book:

How Zippy's was named for the Zip Code.

How ABC came to have stores 50 feet apart.

How Tripler came to be painted pink.

Why Lex Brodie says "thank you very much."

Who the L's were in L&L Drive-Inn.

Who Robert's Hawaii's rabbit logo is waving to and why.

Bob Sevey's stories from the early days of television in the islands.

How the name Meadow Gold was once a butter.

Where the plate lunch came from and how macaroni salad came to be on it.

The Waikiki restaurant Matteo's was founded by Frank Sinatra's touring chef.

237

About The Author

BOB SIGALL IS a life-long entrepreneur. He started his first business in intermediate school, over 30 years ago, filing IRS tax returns for his friends so they would get refunds. For 6 years in high school and college, he had his own window washing business.

Bob has had several businesses since getting his Masters degree from the University of Hawaii in 1975.

He has been a business consultant since 1978 and has owned his own firm, Creative-1, since 1985. Over the years he has offered marketing and management consultation to over 1,000 Hawaii businesses.

In 2004, he launched Management Magic, which provides a mentor to work one-on-one with mid-level managers and supervisors.

Bob has taught marketing at Hawaii Pacific University for 10 years, and these books evolved out of an assignment he gave his students to interview the president of any well-known Hawaii business.

He's a director of Small Business Hawaii and was chairman of their Legislative Action Committee from 1992–2000. In 1997, he co-founded the Business Legislative Coalition.

Bob has been married since 1986 to Lei Honda-Sigall, a parish nurse with St. Francis Healthcare System.

Looking for a speaker for your group?

The author gives talks to community groups about several of the topics in the book. Contact him at:

CompaniesWeKeep@Yahoo.com.

When the new Tripler hospital opened in 1948, it had a stunning view of Salt Lake. Hawaii State Archives photo..